BIO-CULTURAL PROFILE OF DEHRADUN CITY

BIO-CULTURAL PROFILE OF
DEHRADUN CITY

Editors
MADHU BALA SHARMA
V. KAUL

Anthropological Survey of India

SERIALS PUBLICATIONS
NEW DELHI (INDIA)

First Published - 2009

ISBN: 978-81-8387-218-8

Published by

SERIALS PUBLICATIONS
4830/24, Prahlad Street, Ansari Road
Darya Ganj, New Delhi-110002 (India)
Phone : 23245225 Fax : 91-11-23272135
E-mail: serials@satyam.net.in

CONTENTS

LIST OF CONTRIBUTORS

M. M. Srivastava, Head, Department of Botany, D.A.V. (P.G.) College, Dehradun.

G. R. Laxmi, Anthropological Survey of India, Central Regional Centre, Nagpur.

V. K. Sisodia, Department of Sociology, D.A.V. (P.G.) College, Dehradun.

Asha Sisodia, Department of Sociology, K.M.P. (P.G.) College, Dehradun.

Rekha R. Ghosh, Anthropological Survey of India, 27, Jawaharlal Nehru Road, Kolkata.

Swapna Chowdhury, Anthropological Survey of India, Western Regional Centre, Udaipur.

G. S. Bhatt, No. 13, B. N. Chhibbar Marg, Old 11, Arya Nagar, Dehradun.

Zeinab Rehman, Lecturer M. K. P. (P.G.) College, Dehradun.

B. S. N. Bhatnagar, Reader, Department of Economics, D.A.V. (P.G.) College, Dehradun.

H. N. Mishra, D.A.V (P.G.) College, Dehradun.

Vatsala Sarkar, Anthropological Survey of India, North-West Regional Centre, 192/1, Kaulagarh Road, Dehradun.

B. R. Bhatnagar, Anthropological Survey of India, Central Regional Centre, Nagpur.

INTRODUCTION

A Seminar on Bio-Cultural Profile of Dehra Dun city was organized to commemorate the Silver Jubilee Celebrations of the North West Regional Centre. Earlier, seminars on Cultural Profile were held at Kolkata, Mysore, Varanasi, Shillong and Nagpur on the occasion of Silver Jubilee of the respective regional centers. For the first time, a seminar, named Bio-cultural profile of Nagpur City, was organized at Nagpur, in which scholars from both Physical and Cultural anthropology divisions participated. On the same line a seminar on 'Bio-cultural Profile of Dehra Dun City' was organized to commemorate the silver jubilee celebrations of North West Regional Centre in January, 1995. The idea for organizing these seminars was initiated by Dr. S.C. Sinha, former Director, Anthropological Survey of India, who during the seminar at Kolkata, stated that "this effort is to make the social anthropologists, in general and anthropologists in particular, aware about some of the problems involved in systematic understanding of the complex social and cultural reality of the city in which they are residing". It often happens that one knows more about the distant places and things rather than of the immediate surroundings. Though most of us have been living in Dehra Dun for quite some time, it was felt that our knowledge about this city was hardly enough to have even a perspective of the city. Likewise, others must have, their observations from their own vantage points on the city. Then, why we should not get in touch with such people and exchange our notes and see how far we can learn about the place where we live and work. With this idea in mind this seminar was organized under the supervision of the then Head of Office, Dr. (Mrs.) M. B. Sharma, Superintending Anthropologist (P).

Anthropologists are habitually accustomed to study simple and relatively homogeneous communities which may be closely observed in total social and cultural context. When we venture to stretch our interest to a complex and massive social aggregate like the city of Dehra Dun, we would naturally make an effort to organize our research endeavours in terms of a series of observable capsules. It is generally expected that the city's dynamic demand for efficient specialization will cut across the stable lines of kinship, caste and regional loyalty. The anonymities and competitiveness in the city may thus lead to disorganization of traditional ties and release processes of individualization and secularization. In order to regulate an ever growing anonymous population, the city gives rise to a plethora of voluntary associations and formal organizations.

It should thus be obvious that an adequate anthropological picture of the city of Dehra Dun can emerge only out of an endeavour of a large team of devoted field scientists who would be prepared to observe the diverse segments and strata of the city in depth in multiple social contexts of home, neighbourhood, religious festivals, workshops, office, club, political rally and so on. However, the seminar was conducted as a preliminary effort to involve academicians from various fields in this city, as also ourselves, in a systematic understanding of the social and Bio-cultural realities of Dehra Dun city.

Many of the contributors to this seminar were not anthropologists. It was deliberately planned that way so that we anthropologists may expand our horizon out of trying to communicate with academicians and specialists from other disciplines like urban geographers, botanists, environmental scientists, human ecologists, sociologists, folk-artists and specialists from other disciplines.

The organization of such a seminar in Dehra Dun was rewarding experience. Initially we were discouraged by some, about restricting it to Dehra Dun city only. But we got enthusiastic and immediate response from the people when we contacted them for this seminar. As we contacted people our knowledge of the city and its people increased step-by-step. When we initiated the venture we got valuable suggestions and introductions to reach people, and selecting topics for discussions in the seminar was exciting and immensely fruitful. In total we received 15 papers, we were expecting more papers from scholars but due to disturbances on account of Uttarakhand movement we were unable to contact some of the scholars. The selected papers were presented in two academic sessions which were presided over by Prof. R.S. Negi and Dr. M.K. Raha, respectively. Around 12 papers have been included in the present report.

The first session deliberated on papers pertaining to environmental and biocultural aspects of the city, whereas second session discussed socio-cultural scenario of the city.

The first paper deals with the air pollution due to mining, lime industries, automobile exhaust, water pollution because of distillery discharges and domestic sewage. Shri Srivastava has accordingly presented 10 recommendations to check the environmental degradation.

Second paper by G.R. Laxmi deals with the effect of socio-biological factors and ABO incompatibility on differential fertility and mortality among Garhwali Rajputs and Brahmans. Higher education and economic status of the couples result in late marriage. Rajput women attain menarche at a lower age, have higher number of pregnancies and live births, as well as prenatal and post natal deaths than the Brahman women. V.K. Sisodia and Asha Sisodia discuss in detail the demographic profile of Dehra Dun city, throwing light on major ethnic groups and their distribution in the city. B.R. Bhatnagar enumerates the dermatoglyphic variation among Pasi population and discusses the effect of migration and subsequent isolation, if any, of the population. Raj Pasi seem to differ from other sub groups due to low frequencies of loops. But Arch/whorl and whorl/loop index show reverse trend of each other. Swapna Chowdhury did not find any significant difference between Garhwali Brahmin and Rajput population with regard to age, sex structure and fertility, which can be due to similar socio-economic environment. High menarchial age and high rate of adoption of family planning methods is a distinct feature of these populations.

Rekha Rani Ghosh discusses the growth pattern and nutritional status of Garhwali Rajput and Brahmin girls of 6 to 10 years of age. Both the populations show same trend though magnitude of growth differs in the two populations. In the initial years (6-8 years), Brahman girls are taller and heavier but thereafter Rajput girls have greater increments to be taller and heavier than Brahman girls. Due to non-vegetarian diet Rajput girls have greater arm circumference, but probably due to high consumption of milk and milk products, Brahmin girls have more subcutaneous fat than Rajput girls.

G.S. Bhatt discusses in detail the ethnic origins and ethno-religious mosaic of Dehra Dun city.

Zainab Rehman delineates the communal harmony and peaceful co-existence of Hindu and Muslim communities in the valley based on empirical and case studies.

B.N.S. Bhatnagar traces the history of industrial development of Dehra Dun and discusses the industrial development, its effect on Dehra Dun environment. He enumerates the steps taken by Govt. to regulate industrial growth in view of the 'environmentally fragile zone' of Doon valley. At the end he has emphasized the need for a regional policy and has put forth some recommendations for both industrial growth and at the same time preservation of environment.

G.S. Bhat and S.N. Mishra, trace the establishment of Darbar Sahib and emergence of Dehra Dun and their interlinkages. They discuss elaborately the evolution of *Jhanda Mela* and its significance.

Zainab Rahman discusses the evolution of Muslim marriage system, showing a blend of continuity and change of tradition and modernity.

Vatsala Sarkar enumerates the changing cultural profile of Bannuwals, who were forced to migrate from Pakistan during partition of the country and were rehabilitated in Dehra Dun.

Madhu Bala Sharma
V. Kaul

1

ENVIRONMENTAL PROBLEMS IN DOON VALLEY

M. M. Srivastava

Environment, ecology and pollution are the new buzz words. The environmental problems confront the planet with issues unique in its history, the possibility that the Earth's ozone layer, which protects life on Earth from the Sun's harmful radiation, will become seriously depleted and the gloomy threat of global warming caused by the release of green house gases into the atmosphere. Both issues threaten not only the human species but plants and other animals as well. Both issues require- and are receiving-urgent international action.

Dehradun valley with a high percentage of literates is emerging as an "ecology-conscious conglomerate" in otherwise pollution-ridden surroundings. Dehradun recently came into limelight due to its fast deteriorating environment. It is now facing a number of environmental problems due to domestic sewage, automobile exhausts mining of limestone and pyrites, kilning of lime stone and effluent discharge from sugar factory and a molasses distillery. The valley is a closed saucer-shaped area about 70 km long east-west and 20 km wide north-south. It is because of the shape of the valley that the air pollutants cannot rise into the atmosphere and disperse but lie as a thick pall above the trees slowly seeping downward, choking the once abundant foliage. The present paper deals with some important environmental problems in Doon valley.

MINING

Mining is one of the main causes of ecological degradation and environmental imbalance. This industry is next to agriculture and is spread throughout the world. The area of land disturbed by mining is approximately 3,86,000 ha/yr. The two important mineral resources of this region are high grade limestone and rock phosphate (pyrite), the latter being directly used as a phosphatic fertilizer. The mining operations left aside areas which are difficult to restore and show signs of environmental degradtion.

Few years ago more than 50 limestone mines were in operation. These have caused deforestation in the area, especially Musssorie. From a distance it appears as a big scar on the face of Mussoorie hills. Environmental impact of mining reflected in loss of surface vegetation besides contamination of drinking water, drying up of streams and canals and the loss of top soil which nature builds up slowly. Citizens of Dehradun and Mussoorie have recently won a landmark case against powerful mine owners forcing the closure of 54 limestone mines. Eco-task force engineered by ex-soldiers is doing plantation on a large scale to revegetate the area. Nehru Yuvak Kendra did tree plantation at Sahastradhara to stablise the soil.

Open cast rock phosphate mining being done in Dehradun valley at Maldeota, has destroyed the natural vegetation. Destruction of vegetation has made the area highly prone to landslides besides being a source of pollution to the nearby Bindal river which provides drinking water to Dehradun town. Pyrites Phosphates and Chemicals Limited (PPCL), Dehradun, in collaboration with the scientists of F.R.I., have endeavoured to reclaim and afforest the open cast mining area at Maldeota.

LIME INDUSTRY

Lime industry is one of the oldest and biggest cottage industries in Dehradun. There are nearly 200 lime kilns which have become serious threat to the environment. The calcination process of limestone in the lime kilns leads to the emission of a number of gaseous pollutants including carbon dioxide, carbon monoxide and sulphur dioxide. The dust resulting from packing and transportation of finished products form the particulate pollutants (Srivastava and Asha, 1986). Field survey of the area around the lime kilns showed deposition of lime dust on leaf surfaces, flowers and fruits of different plants. Defoliation was observed in *Dalbergia sisoo*. Trees of *Psidium quajara* and *Citrus maxima* exhibited poor growth. For a more comprehensive study of the effect of lime kiln pollutants, plants like *Triticum aestivum*, *Litchi chinensis* and *Cajanus cajan* were studied in detail.

The result of the case studies, carried out in the area, reveal that crops like *Triticum aestivum* (wheat) and *Cajanus cajan* (Arhar) have undergone reduction in chlorophyll content, phytomass, yield parameter and grain quality along with morphological variations. The fruits of *Litchi cheinensis* (Litchi) have low edible part content (pulp). Litchi being an evergreen tree has most of the dust laden leaves. The accumulation of lime dust disrupts physiological process to a high degree resulting in low yield of edible parts. A general survey of the lime kiln area reveals that the inhabitants of these areas suffer from disorders like breathing trouble, bronchitis, cataract, etc.

AUTOMOBILE EXHAUSTS

Dehradun city is now-a-days facing air pollution problems due to a large number of automobiles including three wheelers which are vomiting black smoke causing suffocation and respiratory trouble. The annual mean concentration of suspended particulate matter (SPM) in microgramme per cubic metre is very high (596) in Dehradun, ranking first in India. Dehradun which was earlier considered a paradise for retired persons is now highly polluted.

HYDROLOGICAL PROBLEMS

Hydrological problems that the valley faces emerged from a molasses distillery and domestic sewage. Kuanwala distillery is situated 13 km from Dehradun on Dehradun–Hardwar road. Its product is chiefly country liquor. Distillery discharges large quantities of liquid waste (spent wash) into the river Dholani. During its course to Dholani it pollutes the soil of the surrounding agricultural land due to seepage and overflow. Analysis of the effluents reveals that it is highly acidic in nature (ph. 4.0) and contains high amount of organic and inorganic nutrients. Physio-chemical and biological characteristics of the effluents show that it is toxic in nature and has poor species diversity. The presence of cyanophycean members in high percentage indicates the highly polluted conditions. The plants growing in the vicinity of distillery show scorchy appearance and yellowing of leaves. The study conducted at our laboratory (Renu Rani, 1988) indicated that dilution of the effluent brings down the toxic effect and suitably diluted effluent could be used as a fertilizer for the crops. Water pollution caused by distillery waste in Song and Suswa rivers has led to several fish species migrating elsewhere.

A major portion of domestic sewage is used for irrigation purposes by the farmers and the remaining waste water is thrown out into the river Bindal. As there is no treatment plant available in Dehradun municipality, the sewage waste is thrown out without treatment. Our study reveals that the sewage water is highly polluted. It is highly toxic because of the presence of heavy metals (Augusthy, 1993). Pure sewage has adverse effect on seed germination but its dilution (30%) enhances seed germination. Sewage water at 30% concentration is beneficial for both morphological and ecophysiological variations of *Oryza sativa* (rice) and at 75% is beneficial for *Brassica obracea* (cabbage).

RECOMMENDATIONS

The process of exploitation of environment through industrialization will continue until some concrete steps are taken to stop the onslaught on environment in Doon Valley. The following recommendations are being suggested:

1. The lime kilns which exist in the pocketed area may not have unfavourable effects on plants if they are scattered in some remote areas away from orchards and farms of cultivated plants.

2. Kilns with higher chimneys should be designed to avoid higher concentration of dispersed pollutants near the tree canopies and at ground level.
3. Use of more efficient dust collecting devices should be encouraged to prevent particulate matter dispersion in the ambient air.
4. Growth of resistant varieties of plants should be encouraged around the industrial area. Selection of resistant crop varieties should be undertaken before encouraging their plantation in the industrial belt.
5. The distillery effluent is toxic to the growth of aquatic and terrestrial plants as such the effluent should be diluted at the first outlet point. This process will save the plants from adverse effects of the effluents and at the same time the properly diluted effluent can serve as an additional source of fertilizer.
6. The spent wash from molasses distillery is a potential source of inorganic substances which are highly valuable as a source of nutrient materials. By-product recovery is an efficient process to decrease the pollution load and at the same time it is also economical.
7. Disposal of the diluted effluent over agricultural farms for irrigation and as manure is one of the best practical methods for the disposal of distillery waste.
8. Sewage waste left upon without its treatment must be treated out before it joins with the river.
9. Sewage must be diluted at the first outlet point so that farmers using it for irrigation purposes may be benefited.
10. Indicator value of various algal species present in polluted and non-polluted areas can prove to be of great significance in evaluating the quality of water.

REFERENCES

Augusthy, P.O. (1993), *Ecophysiological responses of Rice* (Oryza sativa var. T3) and *Cabbage* (Brassica oleraceae var. capitata) *to domestic sewage wastes in Dehradun.* D. Phil Thesis, H.N.B. Garhwal University, Srinagar, (Garhwal)-submitted.

Renu Rani (1988), *Effect of Distillery Waste on Ecophysiological Study of Phytoplanktonic and Terrestrial Flora of Dehradun.* D. Phil Thesis, Garhwal University, Srinagar (Garhwal).

Srivastava, M.M. And Asha Rajvanshi (1986), *Effect of Smoke and Lime Dust on some Economic Plants of Surrounding Area of Limestone Kilns at Dehradun.* Final Technical Report, UGC sponsored Research Project, Department of Botany, D.A.V. College, Dehradun.

2

REPRODUCTIVE PERFORMANCES OF THE BRAHMIN AND THE RAJPUT WOMEN IN DEHRADUN CITY

G. R. Laxmi

Growth of a population is governed by several factors, of which fertility is the most important. Fertility is influenced by several socio-biological variables. In depth studies on differential fertility due to social and cultural factors have been carried out by Farlay (1970) and Mommsan (1973). An inverse relationship has been reported between the educational level and fertility of the spouses by different authors. (Chandresekharan, 1961; Li, 1973; Chouhan, 1974; Okodiji, 1974; Nayar, 1974; Gupta et al., 1975; Frinsancho *et al.*, 1976; Khalifa, 1976). There are several reports on fertility and its relationhip with socio-economic conditions of the couples (Sanyal, 1957; Agarwala, 1964; Jain, 1964; Jain, 1970).

Despite several previous studies, whether ABO incompatibility causes differential fertility remained unsolved. Since Hirszfeld's (1925) study on the selective loss of infants, who were incompatible with their mother's ABO blood groups, Matsunaga and Itoh (1958) were the first to study fertility, blood groups and selection on a large scale. This study was followed by Morton and Chung (1959), Newcombe (1963), Reed et al. (1963), Morton *et al.* (1965), Cohan (1970), Hiraizumi (1973), Glegg (1979) etc. Few studies of this kind are available on Indian populations i.e., Sanghvi (1952), Reddy and Reddy (1977), Chakravarti and Chakravarti (1978), Satyanarayana *et al.* (1978), Jindal and Basu (1981), Jindal *et al.*, (1983) etc.

In the present communication, an attempt has been made to study the differential fertility and mortality vis-à-vis some of the socio-biological factors as well as the effects of ABO incompatibility on differential fertility and mortality. For this study, two endogamous population groups namely the Rajput and the Brahmins of Uttar Pradesh have been studied.

MATERIAL AND METHOD

The data collection among the 110 Rajput and the 92 Brahmin women has been carried out through questionnaires during May 1981—September, 1982 in different phases under the An.S.I. Sponsored research project entitled 'A study of differential fertility, matarnofetal incompatibility and congenital malformations in Dehradun city' from Government women hospital, Dehradun (U.P). Doon Valley is situated at 29°57′ and 31°21′ north latitude and 77°35′ and 78°29′east longitude. The altitude of the valley is about 791 meters and the climate is moderate. The information regarding socio-economic and educational status of spouses, age and menarche, age at marriage, use of birth control devices, fertility and mortality were obtained directly from women of different economic strata. The necessary information thus obtained was cross checked with the husband or any other female member of the family. Induced abortions were not included in the present study.

Blood samples from wife and husband were collected from finger tip and for new born, the cord blood was taken. The blood samples were analysed for ABO blood groups following standard technique of testing. Conventional statistical measures have been used for analysing the data and drawing inferences thereof on various parameters.

RESULTS AND DISCUSSION

Information on reproductive performance of 110 Rajput women and 92 Brahmin women were collected for the present communication. The overall rate of pregnancies of the Rajput and Brahmin is 2.73 and 2.37 respectively (Table 1). The Rajput women display higher mean estimates than the Brahmin women. The data have been classified in terms of the age group of woman in order to study the trend. An apparent trend of higher mean estimates is noticeable for all the events as the mother's age increases (Figure 1). In both the populations, postnatal deaths (children upto five years of age) are mainly caused due to diarrhoea, congenital heart disease, pneumonia, typhoid, respiratory problems, prematurity etc.

Table 1
Mean of Reproductive Events of the Brahmin Women

Age group of women (years)	*No.*	*Pregnancies*	*Live births*	*Living children*	*Prenatal deaths*	*Postnatal deaths*
15-19	9	1.5555	1.2222	1.1111	0.3333	0.1111
20-24	41	1.7073	1.6097	1.5366	0.0976	0.0732
25-29	35	2.9143	2.5143	2.4143	2.3143	0.2286
30 and above	7	4.2857	3.8571	3.2857	0.2857	0.7143
Total	92	2.3696	2.1522	1.9674	0.2174	0.1848

Table 1A
Mean of Reproductive Events of the Rajput Women

Age group of women (years)	*No.*	*Pregnancies*	*Live births*	*Living children*	*Prenatal deaths*	*Postnatal deaths*
15-19	10	1.1000	1.1000	1.000	-	0.1000
20-24	52	1.8846	1.7674	1.6538	0.1731	0.0769
25-29	31	3.3636	2.9032	2.6129	0.4193	0.2581
30 - 34	9	5.5714	4.6667	4.1667	0.3333	0.8889
35 and above	8	5.7500	4.6250	4.3750	1.0000	0.2500
Total	110	2.7273	2.4273	2.2182	0.3000	0.2091

The number of children borne by a woman in her life time is influenced by various cultural and biological factors. Cultural components of fertility are governed by societal norms, which vary from society to society. Biological factors of fertility depend on certain biological events. Thus, fertility has

*Figure-1: **Reproductive Events of Brahmin and Rajput Women***

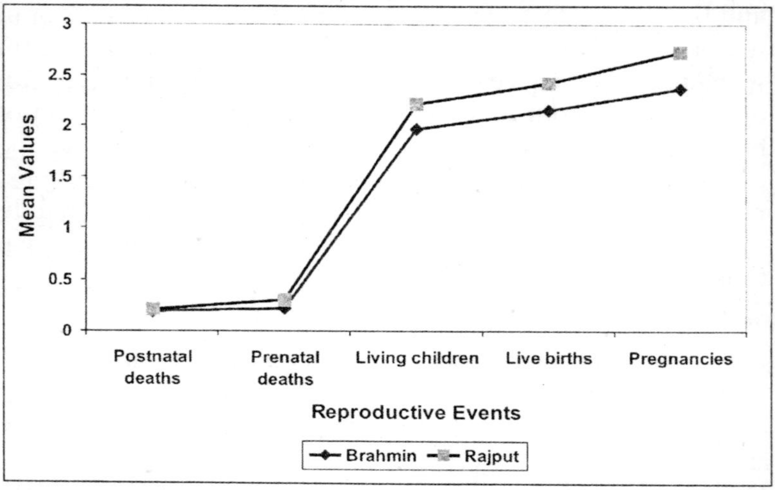

multifactorial evidence and is influenced by education and economic status of couples, age at menarche, age at marriage etc.

The education has emerged as one of the important effects on fertility. Evidence of an inverse relationship between fertility and education as well as economic status is well established. The increase in educational level also tends to increase the age at marriage and thus, reducing the exposure to fertility (Chouhan, 1974). The educational status of the wives and husbands has been divided into the categories (i) no formal education (ii) middle school (iii) secondary school (iv) graduate level and above (Table 2). The mean age at marriage for the Brahmin men and women are 24.40 years and 18.77 years respectively. The means are 23.56 years and 18.08 years for the Rajput men and women respectively. It has been observed that among the Brahmin as well as Rajput men and women, age at marriage gradually increased with an increase in their educational status (Figure 2 and 3).

The women educated up to secondary level married significantly later than the women with no formal education among the Brahmins (t = 5.1601 P<0.001). Likewise men educated upto graduate level among the Brahmins are reported to have married significantly at later stages than their uneducated counterparts (t=3.2845, 0.01>P>0.001). Among the Rajputs, women educated up to secondary level marry significantly later than the women with no formal education (t = 4.9188, P<0.001). Rajput men educated up to graduate level marry later than the men with no formal education, however, the results are statistically not significant (t = 1.4790. P>0.2.1). Previous surveys conducted in Kanpur, Madras, Calcutta, Lucknow and Delhi have also revealed that females who marry late have less number of children than those who marry early (Majumdar, 1955; Balakrishna, 1961; Mukherjee, 1962; Saksena, 1962; Agarwala , 1970).

Table 2
Age at Marriage According to Educational Status of Men and Women

Educational status	*Brahmin*		*Rajput*	
	No.	*Age at Marriage Mean ± S.E.*	*No.*	*Age at Marriage Mean ± S.E.*
Men				
1. No formal education	3	22.2500 ± 0.9859	21	22.7143 ± 0.8787
2. Middle School	17	22.3333 ± 0.7984	30	22.9333 ± 0.8441
3. Secondary School	42	23.4815 ± 0.9343	37	23.5946 ± 0.5103
4. Graduate	17	26.2353 ± 0.7098	13	24.4615 ± 0.7895
5. Postgraduate and above	13	26.3846 ± 0.8589	9	26.2222 ± 0.5720
Total	92	24.4022 ± 0.4047	110	23.5636 ± 0.3536
Women				
1. No formal education	22	16.3636 ± 0.5681	53	16.8679 ± 0.3066
2. Middle School	22	17.4091 ± 0.4909	16	17.5625 ± 0.5914
3. Secondary School	30	20.000 ± 0.4180	29	19.5172 ± 0.4428
4. Graduate & above	18	21.3333 ± 0.6860	12	20.6667 ± 0.6316
Total	92	18.7717 ± 0.3239	110	18.0818 ± 0.2543

The fertility of women in each group according to educational status is measured in terms of mean number of live births. The mean number of live births among the illiterate woman of Brahmin and Rajputs are 2.77 and 2.73 respectively and found to decrease with the increase in the educational level (Table 3). Mean number of live births categorised according to educational level of Brahmin and Rajput men also show a

Figure-2: **Educational Status and Age at Marriage (Men)**

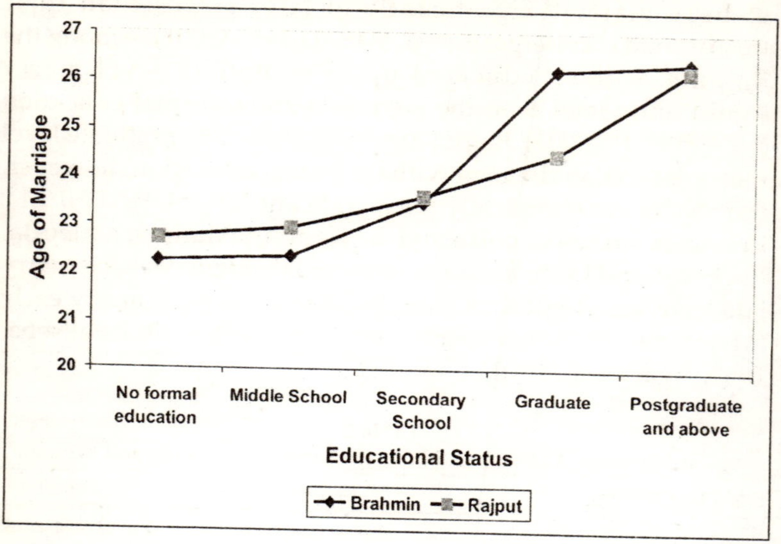

Figure-3: **Educational Status and Age at Marriage (Women)**

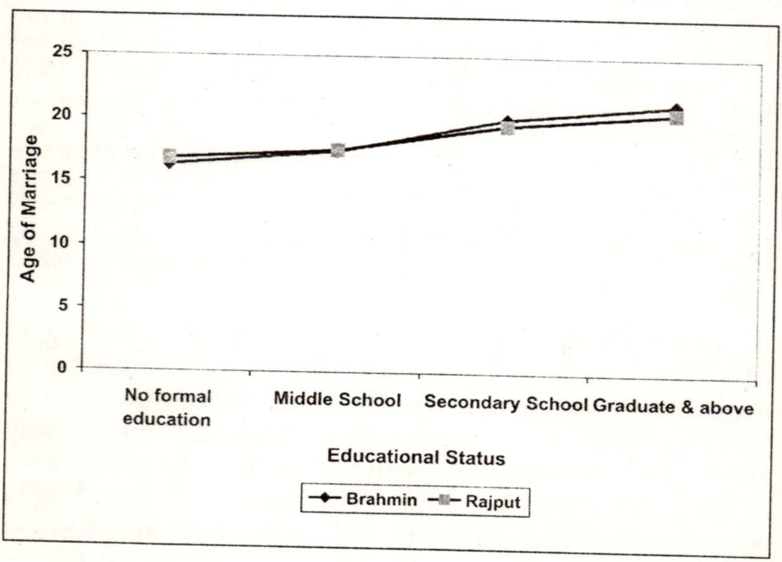

similar trend of decrease, however, the results are statistically not significant at 5% level of probability, except the Brahmin women who are reported to have significantly lower mean number of live births among the women with secondary education than the women with no formal education (t=2.8033, 0.01>P>0.001). Thus, education up to graduate level for men and high school level for women is effective to increase the age at marriage and to reduce the fertility. Increase in educational status of men and women not only increase their age at marriage but also increase the birth control device users as well as they adopt induced abortions as birth control, if necessary.

Table 3
Fertility According to Educational Status of Men and Women

Educational Status	*Brahmin*		*Rajput*	
	No.	*Live births Mean + S.E.*	*No.*	*Live births Mean + S.E.*
Men				
1. No formal education	3	2.3333 + 0.3333	21	2.7619 + 0.4018
2. Middle School	17	2.8750+ 0.3521	30	2.7667 + 0.3413
3. Secondary School	42	2.0000 + 0.1738	37	2.2703 + 0.2074
4. Graduate and above	30	1.7333 + 0.1585	22	1.9545 + 0.2415
Total	92	2.1522 + 0.1170	110	2.4273 + 0.1468
Women				
1. No formal education	22	2.7727 + 0.2786	53	2.7358 + 0.2351
2. Middle school	22	2.2727 + 0.2296	16	2.4375 + 0.3648
3. Secondary School	30	1.8333 + 0.1862	29	2.1724 + 0.2435
4. Graduate and above	18	1.7778 + 0.1905	12	1.5833 + 0.3128

Another factor, likely to be related to fertility is the economic condition. Economic status of spouses has been grouped into four broad categories on the basis of monthly per capita income as shown in Table 4. Increase in economic status tends to increase the age at marriage for both men and women of Brahmin and Rajput (Figure 4 and 5). Brahmin women reported to have significantly higher age at marriage among the highest per capita income group than the women from the category II (t = 3.4086; 0.01>P> 0.001). Similarly Rajput women of highest per capita income group observed significantly higher age at marriage than the women of lowest

Table 4
Age at Marriage in Various Per Capita Income Groups

	Brahmin								Rajput							
		Age at marriage								Age at marriage						
		Husband			Wife					Husband			Wife			
Percapita income (Rs.)	*N*	*Mean*	±	*S.E.*	*Mean*	±	*S.E.*		*N*	*Mean*	±	*S.E.*	*Mean*	±	*S.E.*	
< 50	-	-		-					67	23.2439	±	1.1097	16.8333	±	0.6009	
50 - 200	35	24.0545	±	0.6321	18.0364	±	0.3787		75	23.8333	±	0.4090	17.4800	±	0.2942	
201 - 350	29	25.2069	±	0.5688	19.1379	±	0.5222		19	24.2143	±	0.7572	19.5789	±	0.5313	
> 350	8	26.3750	±	1.2092	22.5000	±	1.2536		8	25.5000	±	0.5345	20.7500	±	0.7962	
Total	92	24.4026	±	0.4355	18.7717	±	0.3239		110	23.5636	±	0.3536	18.0826	±	0.2499	

Figure-4: **Economy and Age at Marriage (Men)**

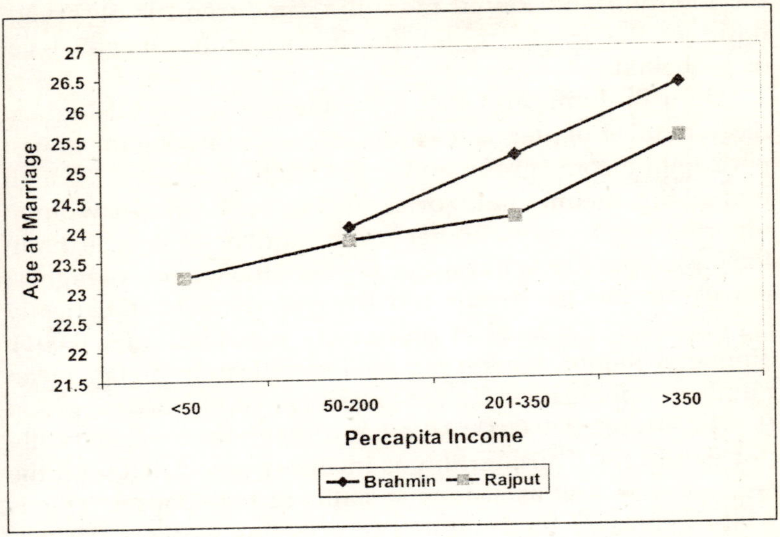

Figure-5: **Economy and Age at Marriage (Women)**

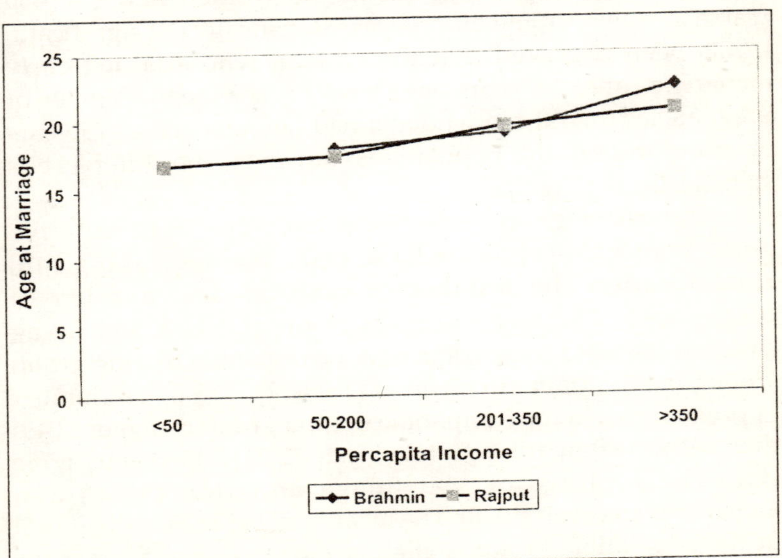

per capita income group (t = 3.9285; 0.01> P>0.001). Among the Brahmin and Rajput men, the same trend is observed; however, the results are statistically not significant at 5% level of probability.

Both Brahmin and Rajput women experienced highest mean number of pregnancies and live births among the lowest per capita income group and it gradually decreased through increasing income categories (Table 5). Brahmin women reported significantly higher mean number of live births in the lowest per capita income group than the women of highest per capita income group and the difference is statistically significant at 5% level of probability (t = 4.9229; P< 0.001). Similarly, Rajput women reported significantly higher mean number of pregnancies in the lowest per capita income group (t = 3.2394; 01>P>0.001). All other differences are statistically not significant. Thus, fertility is inversely associated with the education as well as economic status of the spouses. This is well established by a number of previous workers (Driver, 1963; Jain, 1975; Agarwala, 1964).

The mean menarchial age of the Brahmin women is higher 15.45 ± 0.3371 than that of the Rajput women 14.8 ± 0.1450 (Table 6), however, the difference is statistically not significant. It has been observed that the women who attained early menarche (upto 14 years age) have higher mean number of pregnancies than those who attained late menarche (15 years or more) in both the populations; however, the difference is statistically not significant.

ABO blood group incompatibility: The reproductive performances of spouses have been studied taking into consideration the number of matings and number of pregnancies. The mean number of pregnancies and living children for ABO compatible and incompatible mating group among the Brahmin are given in (Table 7). The mean number of pregnancies in the compatible mating group is higher (2.49) than in the incompatible mating group (2.21). The results agree with the findings of Matsunaga and Itoh (1958) and Satyanarayana et al; (1978). The mean number of living children in the compatible group is slightly more as compared to the

Table 5
Fertility in various percapita income groups

Per capita income group (Rs.)	Brahmin						Rajput					
	Pregnancies			Live births			Pregnancies			Live births		
	Mean	±	S.E.	Mean	±	S.E.	Mean	±	S.E.	Mean	±	S.E.
< 50		-			-		3.5714	±	0.7514	3.5714	±	0.7514
50 - 200	2.6545	±	0.1928	2.4182	±	0.1719	2.9367	±	0.2136	2.5443	±	0.1734
201 - 350	2.0345	±	0.2134	1.7241	±	0.1561	2.2000	±	0.2619	2.0000	±	0.2390
> 350	1.6250	±	0.4199	1.2500	±	0.1637	1.1111	±	0.1111	1.0000	±	0.0
Total	2.3696	±	0.1423	2.1522	±	0.1170	2.7273	±	0.1724	2.4273	±	0.1468

Table 6
Mean Number of Pregnancies According to Age at Menarche

Age at menarche (years)	*Brahman*				*Rajput*			
	N	*Pregnancies*	±	*S.E.*	*N*	*Pregnancies*	±	*S.E.*
11 & 12	-				3	3.0000	±	1.0000
13	14	2.2143	±	0.3805	13	3.3077	±	0.4721
14	18	2.5555	±	0.3544	35	3.0000	±	0.3305
15	21	2.1428	±	0.2698	27	2.4444	±	0.3594
16	24	2.5000	±	0.2823	21	2.6190	±	0.3483
17 & 18	15	2.4667	±	0.3763	11	1.8182	±	0.3252
Early menarche upto 14 yrs.	32	2.4062	±	0.2574	51	3.0784	±	0.2569
Late menarche 15 yrs. and above	60	2.3667	±	0.1715	59	2.3898	±	0.2131

Table 7
Distribution of Pregnancies and Living Children in Different ABO Mating Types among the Brahmin

	Pregnancies				*Living children*			
Mating type	*No. of matings*	*Mean*	±	*S.E.*	*No. of matings*	*Mean*	±	*S.E.*
Compatible matings								
A X A	5	3.6000	±	0.8124	5	2.8000	±	0.4899
B X B	8	2.1250	±	0.6105	8	1.8750	±	0.3981
AB X AB	–	–			–		–	
A X O	15	2.5333	±	0.3763	15	1.9333	±	0.2839
B X O	7	2.1428	±	0.3401	7	1.8771	±	03401
AB X O	1	2.0000	±	0000	1	2.0000	±	0000
AB X A	6	3.0000	±	0.6831	6	2.3333	±	0.6667
AB X B	1	3.0000	±	0000	1	2.0000	±	0000
O X O	11	2.1818	±	0.3521	11	1.7273	±	0.2727
Total	54	2.4905	±	0.1954	54	2.0000	±	0.1458
Incompatible matings								
O X A	4	2.2857	±	0.5216	4	1.7143	±	0.3595
O X B	8	2.4000	±	0.3712	8	1.9231	±	0.2878
O X AB	2	1.5000	±	0.5000	2	1.5000	±	0.5000
A X B	6	2.6667	±	0.6667	6	2.0000	±	0.4472
B X A	6	2.1667	±	0.6540	6	2.000	±	0.5164
A X AB	3	1.6667	±	0.6667	3	1.6667	±	0.6667
B X AB	4	1.1500	±	0.2500	4	1.2500	±	0.2500
Total	38	2.2105	±	0.2036	38	1.8158	±	0.1594

incompatible group (2.00 and 1.81 respectively). Both these differences are statistically not significant (t = 0.9925, 0.4>P>0.3 and t = 0.8532; 0.47> P>0.3) respectively.

Among the Rajput (Table 8), the mean number of pregnancies in the ABO compatible mating group is 2.06 and it is 2.77 among the incompatible mating group. The mean number of living children is higher (2.32) in the compatible mating group than in the incompatible mating group (2.06). Both the differences are statistically not significant (t = 0.2961; 0.8>P>0.7 and t = 1.0761; 0.2>P>0.1) respectively.

Table 8
Distribution of Pregnancies and Living Children in Different ABO Mating Types among the Rajput

	Pregnancies				Living children			
Mating type	*No. of matings*	*Mean*	*±*	*S.E.*	*No. of matings*	*Mean*	*±*	*S.E.*
Compatible matings								
A X A	11	1.8182	±	0.4635	11	1.7273	±	0.4283
B X B	7	2.2500	±	0.4767	7	2.1250	±	0.5489.
AB X AB	1	1.0000			1.	1.0000		
A X O	13	2.9231	±	0.4594	13	2.8461	±	0.4783
B X O	8	2.7500	±	0.6478	8	2.1250	±	0.4795
AB X O	3	2.3333	±	0.3333	3	2.3333	±	0.3333
AB X A	3	2.2333	±	0.6667	3	2.0000	±	0.5754
AB X B	6	2.6000	±	0.5010	6	2.2200	±	0.3742
O X O	9	3.6222	±	0.7663	9	3.1111	±	0.5122
Total	61	2.6610	±	0.2689	61	2.3226	±	0.1836
Incompatible matings								
O X A	8	3.4286	±	1.0202	8	2.4286	±	0.4809
O X B	11	2.4444	±	0.5031	11	2.0000	±	0.3944
O X AB	4	2.5000	±	0.6455	4	2.2500	±	0.4787
A X B	10	3.4000	±	0.9333	10	2.1000	±	0.4060
B X A	9	2.5000	±	0.5000	9	1.6250	±	0.3750
A X A B	2	2.5000	±	1.5000	2	2.000	±	1.0000
B X AB	5	2.8000	±	0.3742	5	2.4000	±	0.2449
Total	49	2.7755	±	0.2786	49	2.0625	±	0.1571

The percentages of abortions, still births and neo-natal deaths are higher in the ABO incompatible group than the compatible group and consequently the incompatible group reported lower frequency of live births in both the populations (Table 9 A and B). Chi square tests revealed that there is no significant difference between the distribution of abortions, still births, neonatal deaths and live births of ABO compatible and incompatible groups among the Brahmins.

Table 9A
Fertility and Mortality in ABO Compatible and Incompatible Mating Groups among the Brahmin

Mating type	*Fetal deaths (%)*	*Abortions (%)*	*Still birth (%)*	*Naonatal deaths (%)*	*Live births (%)*	*Pregnancies*
ABO (Comp)	16 (10.96)	13 (8.90)	3 (2.05)	4 (2.74)	130 (89.04)	146
ABO (In Comp)	9 (12.33)	7 (9.58)	2 (2.73)	3 (4.11)	64 (87.67)	73

Table 9B
Fertility and Mortality in ABO Compatible and Incompatibe Mating Groups among the Rajput

Mating type	*Fetal deaths (%)*	*Abortions (%)*	*Still birth (%)*	*Naonatal deaths (%)*	*Live births (%)*	*Pregnancies*
ABO (Comp)	15 (9.15)	11 (6.71)	4 (2.44)	3 (1.83)	147 (89.63)	164
ABO (In Comp)	18 (13.23)	15 (11.03)	3 (2.20)	6 (4.41)	116 (85.29)	136

The incidence of abortions, still births and neo-natal deaths has been presented as indices calculated from the frequency of live births. Viability loss index of each mating type includes the total fetal deaths plus neonatal deaths. These indices are calculated, according to Cohen (1970), and are presented in Table 10. It has been observed that the Brahmins exhibit indices of higher values for abortions, still births, neo-natal deaths and viability loss in the ABO incompatible mating group than in the compatible group. Among the Rajputs, it can be noted that the abortion index, total fetal, neonatal and viability loss indices are higher in the ABO incompatible group than in the compatible group. However, still birth index shows higher value in the compatible group than in the incompatible group. Lower indicator ratio (0.9504) for still births indicates that ABO incompatibility disease is more prevalent in late pregnancy, as observed by earlier workers (Cohen, 1970; Lauritsen, 1975). Higher neonatal mortality in ABO incompatible mating is suggestive of the fact that the ABO incompatibility disease might be carried over to the neonatal period (Cohen, 1970). Indicator ratio for the ABO incompatibility effect in case of viability loss index is 1.2187 among the Brahmins and it is 1.6896 among the Rajputs. This indicates the etiological importance of ABO incompatibility in the pregnancy outcome and neonatal mortality. These findings agree with the earlier reports (Cohen, 1970; Jindal *et al.*, 1983).

Table 10

Death Indices and Indicator Ratios for ABO Effect among the Brahmin

Mating type	*No. of pregnancies*	*No. of births*	*Abortion Index*	*Still birth index*	*Total fetal death index*	*Neonatal death index*	*Viability loss index*
ABO compatible	146	130	10.0000	2.3077	12.3077	3.0769	15.3846
ABO incompatible	73	64	10.9375	3.1250	14.0625	4.6875	18.7500
Indicator ratio I/C	-	-	1.0937	1.3542	1.1426	1.5234	1.2187

Table 10A

Death indices and indicator ratios for ABO effect among the Rajput

Mating type	*No. of pregnancies*	*No. of births*	*Abortion Index*	*Still birth index*	*Total fetal death index*	*Neonatal death index*	*Viability loss index*
ABO compatible	164	147	7.4830	2.7211	10.2041	2.0408	12.2449
ABO incompatible	136	116	12.9310	2.5862	15.5172	5.1724	20.6896
Indicator ratio I/C			1.7280	0.9504	1.5207	2.5345	1.6896

Rajputs show higher values of abortion index, total fetal death, neonatal and viability loss index than the Brahmins. Among the Rajputs, ABO incompatible mating group show higher mean number of pregnancies as well as higher mortality, reproductive compensation, thus seems to be operative among the Rajput only. In the present study differential fertility has been studied and found that higher educational and economic status of couple give rise to an increase in mean age at marriage thus reducing the reproductive life span of the couples. Age at menarche is also one of the factors covering differential fertility. Rajput men and women have lower age at marriage than the Brahmin men and women respectively. Rajput women reported lower age at menarche, higher mean member of pregnancies and live births as well as prenatal and postnatal deaths than the Brahman women. In both the populations, the ABO incompatibility effect has been observed, however, it is more pronounced among the Rajputs. This may be due to some other factors besides the ABO incompatibility phenomenon which are influencing the reproductive behaviour of this population vis-à-vis ABO compatibility/incompatibility.

REFERENCE

Agarwala, S.N. (1964), Social and Cultural Factors Affecting Fertility in India. *Population review* 8: 1.

Agarwala, S.N. (1970), A Demographic Study of Six Urbanizing Villages, *New York, Asia Publishing House.*

Bala Krishna, R. (1961), Report on the Economic survey of Madras city 1954-57 New Delhi. Research Programme committee. *Planning Commision*, Pp. 232-33.

Chakravartti and Rama Chakravartti (1978), ABO Blood Groups and Fertility in an Indian Population, *J De Genet. Hum.* 26: 133-44.

Chandrasekharan (1961), *In: Social demography in India.* B.K. Roy (Unpublished Monograph).

Chouhan, J.S. (1974), Age at Marriage: A Study of 400 Mothers obtaining Maternity Services at a Metropolitan Teaching Hospital. *J. Fam. Wel.* 20:40-48.

Glegg, E.J. (1979), Blood Groups and Reproduction in Habrideen Women. *Ann. Hum-Biol.* 6 : 111-129.

Cohen, B.H. and J.E. Sayre (1967), Further Observation on the relationship of maternal ABO and Rh types to fetal death. *Amer. J. Hum. Genet.* 20 : 310-343.

Cohen, B.H. (1970), ABO and Rh incompatibility

(i) Fetal and neonatal mortality: Some new interpretations.

(ii) Is there a dual interaction in combined ABO and Rh incompatibility. *Amer. J. Human. Genet.* 22:412-39 & 441-452.

Driver, E.D. (1963), *Differential Fertility in Central India,* Princeton, *Princeton Univ. Press*, 99-101.

Farley R. (1970), *Growth of the Black Population: A Study of Demographic Trends*, Markham, Chicago.

Frinsancho, A.K., J.E. Khayuman and J. Matros. (1976), Symbolic Relationship of High Fertility, High Childhood Mortality and Socio-economic Status of an Urban Peruvian Population, *Human Biol.* 48: 101-11.

Gupta, K.L., R. Singh and L.H. David (1975), Fertility and Fertility Differential in a Rural Area, We: 21. 3-9.

Hiraizumi Y., C.T. Spradlin, R. Itoh and S.A. Andersno (1973), Frequency of Parental Deaths and its Relationship to the ABO Blood Groups in Man, *Amer. J. Hum. Genet.* 25 : 362-71.

Hirszfeld, L. and H. Zborowski (1925), Gruppenspezifische Beziahunganz-wischen Mutter and frucht and elektive Durchhsigkait der placenta : Klinische Wochen-schrft 4 : 1152-57 c.f. Clegg, E.J. 1979.

Jain, P.K. (1970), Demographic and Socio-economic Characteristics and Development of Family Planning Programme in Mysore State, Seminar on Family Planning in Mysore State.

Jain, S.P. (1964), Indian Fertility: Our Knowledge and Gaps, *J. Fam. Wel. Bomb.* 41(6).

Jain, S.P. (1975), Demography: A Status Study on Population Research in India, Vol. II, New Delhi, Tata Mc Graw Hill Publication.

Jindal, Anil and S.K. Basu, ABO Blood Group Incompatibility Differentials in Reproductive Performance with Respect to Maternal Age and Parity among Dawoodi Bohras of Udaipur Rajastan, *Ind. J. Med. Res.* 74 : 688-95.

Jindal, Anil, S.K. Basu and I.J.S Bansal (1983); A Population Study on ABO-Rh Blood Group Incompatibilities and Prenatal and Neo Natal Mortality, *Ind. J., Med. Res.* 77, 208-12.

Khalifa, A.M. (1976), The Influence of Wife's Education on Fertility in Rural Egypt, *Bio. Soc. Science.* 8 : 53-60.

Lauritsen, J.G. (1975), Incompatibility as a Cause of Spontaneous Abortion, *Clin. Genet.* 7 : 308-16.

Li, W.L. (1973), Temporal and Spatial Analysis of Fertility Decline in Taiwan Population Study. 27(1). Cf. Khalifa, A.M. 1976.

Majumdar, D.N. (1955), *Social Contours of an Industrial City* (Social Survey of Kanpur City, 1954-55) 1960. Bombay, Asia Publishing House.

Matsunaga and Itoh (1958), Blood Groups and Fertility in Japanese Population with Special Reference to Intra-uterine Selection due to Maternal Fetal Incompatibility, *Ann. Hum. Genet.* 22: 111-31.

Mommsen K.G. (1973), Differentials in Fertility among Black Doctorates. *Soc. Biol.* 20 : 20-30.

Morton, N.E. and C.A. Chung (1959), Are the MN Blood Groups Maintained by Selection? *Amer. J. Hum. Genet.* 11: 237-51.

Morton, N.E., H. Kriegar, and M.B. Mi (1966), Natural Selection on Polymorphisms in North Eastern Brazil, *Amer. J. Hum. Genet.* 18: 153-71.

Mukherjee, R.K. and B. Singh (1961), *Social Profiles of a Metropolis Bombay*, Asia Publishing House.

Mukherjee, S.B. (1962), *Studies on Fertility Rates in Calcutta*, Bookland Pvt. Ltd.

Nayar, P.K.B. (1974), The Influence of Education on Fertility, *J. Famil. Wel.* 20: 28-36.

Newcombe, H.B. (1963), Risk of Fetal Death to Mothers of Different ABO and Rh Blood Types, *Amer. J. Hum. Genet.* 15: 449-64.

Okadiji, F. (1974), Changes in individual reproductive behaviour and cultural values. In, Lecture services in population. *International Union for the Scientific study of population*, Bucharest, World Population Year.

Rami Reddy, V. and B.K. Chandrasekhar Reddy (1977), ABO Blood Group Mating Types and Fertility among the Reddis of Chittoor district, Andhra Pradesh. *The Anthropologist*. 24: 46-55.

Reed, T.E., H. Garshowitz, A. Soni and J. Napier (1963), A Search for Natural Selection in Six Blood Group Systems and ABO Secretion. *Amer. J. Hum. Genet.* 16: 161-79

Sanghvi, L.D. (1951), ABO Blood Groups and Sex-ratio at Birth in Man: Nature (London) 168: 1077.

Sanyal, S.N. (1957), Factors Affecting Fertility, *Man in India*. 37. 268-79.

Satyanarayana, M., M. Vijayalakshmi, C. Sambasiva Rao and Mathew Susan (1978), ABO Blood Groups and Fertility with Special Reference to Intra Uterine Selection due to Materno Fetal Incompatibility, *Amer. J. Phy. Anthrop. J.*, 49. 389-95.

Sexena, G.B. (1962), Age and Marriage and Fertility. A Sample Study in the Rural

3

DEMO-ETHNIC STRUCTURE OF DEHRADUN CITY

Vijay Sisodia & Asha Sisodia

Residential clustering of people with similar socio-cultural and economic attributes is a universal feature of cities all over the world. It is a reflection not only of ethnic solidarity and prejudices among the various social groups, but of a special manifestation of the prevailing social inequalities also. Indian cities are no exception to this general law of residential segregation. Historically, cities in India have displayed a type of residential segregation where various castes, regional and religious groups reside in clearly demarcated localities of enclaves (Vishwanadham, 1986). According to Mukherjee (1968), every urban center used to contain a large number of natural areas which are formed on the basis of caste, race, occupation or religion. Multi-relgious and multi-lingual urban centers provide greater possibilities for the emergence of more complex pattern of ethnic and ecological segregation and there is hardly any large Indian city whose population structure is not organized along these lines.

During the last few decades a number of sociologists, anthropologists, demographers and geographers have carried out a number of studies on ethnic and ecological structure of third world cities. Unfortunately, in India this aspect of urban social structure has not drawn the desired attention of sociologists and social anthropologists. Leaving apart few exceptions (Vishwanandham, 1986; Mehata, 1968; Bose, 1986; Ghosh, 1950; Gist, 1958 etc.) extremely limited literature is available on ethnic structure and residential segregation in Indian cities. This is indeed disappointing and is due to the fact that researches on the city have not been on the priority list of sociologists and social anthropologists. The present paper is an attempt to fill this gap in urban studies. It attempts to describe the demographic profile of Dehradun city along with its ethnic composition on the basis of prevailing residential segregation in the city. As the data on residential segregation is hardly available, the analysis is based on personal observations and interviews with key respondents from various ethnic groups. The paper is divided into two parts– part one deals with the demographic structure of Dehradun and the part two presents the ethnic composition and the patterns of residential segregation.

Dehradun, the gateway of Uttarakhand and the headquarter of the district is situated in the Doon valley. It is located between 77°35′ and 78°20′ east longitude and 29°57′ and 31°20′ north latitude. The city is surrounded by river Song on the east and river Asan in the west; lesser Himalayan ranges in the north and the sal forests of Shivalik ranges in the south. The city is located at an altitude of 640 meters above mean sea level. The lowest altitude is 600 meters in the southern part, whereas the highest altitude is 1000 meters on the northern part of the city.

The name of the city is composed of two words 'DEHRA' and 'DOON'. Dehra appears to be a corruption of 'Dera' signifying a temporay abode or camp and 'Doon' means a valley. During the 17th century the Sikh Guru Ram Rai, who belonged to the sect of Udasi Fakirs, took up his residence or camp in Doon and the place came to be known as Dehradun. Some historians think that 'Dehrad' combines two Hindi words 'Deh' (Body) and 'Hara' (lost). Since Guru Ram Rai lost his life here in the 'Doon' so the place was called Dehradun (Gupta, 1986). The Dehradun city took its modern shape with the arrival of Britishers during the 19th century. The calm and quite atmosphere, lush green surroundings and moderate climate lured a number of retired British and Indian Civil servant and army officers to come here and settle permanently. This prompted Ruskin Bond to call Dehradun a city of grey hairs and green hedges.

Today, Dehradun though small in size, commands a national importance in many ways. It can be proud of its premier scientific and research institutions such as Anthropological Survey of India, Archaeological Survey of India, Botanical Survey of India, Central soil and Water Conservation Research and Training Institute, Defence Electronic Application Laboratory, Forest Research Intitute and College, Indian Bureau of Mines, Indian Institute of Petroleum, Indian Photo Interpretation Institute, Instrumentation Research and Development Establishment, Ordnance Factory, Naval Hydrographic Office, National Institute of Visually Handicapped, Oil and Natural Gas Corporation Ltd., K.D. Malvia Institute of Petroleum Exploration, Survey of India, Wild Life Institute of India, Wadia Institute of Himalayan Geology and Zoological Survey of India etc. These scientific and research institutions well deservedly called the 'corporate citizens' have given Dehradun an honoured place at national and international level. Apart from this, Dehradun also has the highest density of public schools in the country. Some of these schools are not only of national but of international fame such as Doon School and Welham Girls School. So Dehradun may rightly be called a scientific and literary town of not only Uttar Pradesh but of whole northern India.

DEHRADUN: A DEMOGRAPHIC PROFILE

The demographic profile constitutes a crucial variable in understanding the social and ethnic structure of a city. As both these aspects of urban population are not constant, they undergo changes as a result of growth in population size and changes in its composition.

Dehradun is the twelfth largest city among class I cities of U.P. according to the size of population (Master Plan, 1982). According to 1981 census, the total population of Dehradun urban agglomeration was 2, 53,628 persons and that of

Municipal area was 2,11,838 persons. Table 1 shows the absolute figures of population, increase of popuation and the percentage decinal increase from 1901 to 1981 for urban agglomeration and the municipal area of Dehradun. The decade 1941-1951 is most important in the population growth in Dehradun, as the Municipal area of Dehradun registered a decinal growth of 95.52 per cent. This increase can be attributed to the huge influx of refugees to India from Pakistan. The number of displaced persons in the Dehradun district at the time of census of 1951 was 48,080 persons, a large majority of whom were concentrated in urban areas. Dehradun ranks seventh among Class I cities of U.P. in the rate of population growth during the decade 1971-81.

Table 1
Population Growth of Dehradun 1901-1981

Year	*Dehradun urban agglomertion*			*Dehradun municipal area*		
	Population	*Decinal*	*Percentage Increase*	*Population Increase*	*Decinal Increase*	*Percentage Increase*
1901	30,995	-	-	30,995	-	-
1911	42,568	11,573	+37.34	42,568	11,573	+37.34
1921	50,828	8,290	+19.47	50,858	8,290	+11.47
1931	52,927	2,066	+4.17	43,206	7,652	-15.05
1941	90,580	27,653	+52.25	59,535	16,323	+37.69
1951	144,216	63,636	+78.97	116,404	56,869	+95.52
1961	156,341	12,125	+8.41	126,918	10,514	+9.03
1971	203,464	47,123	+30.14	166,073	39,115	+30.85
1981	293,628	90.164	+44.31	211,838	55,765	+33.58

Source: Master Plan for Dehradun 1982-2001

The comparative figures of age groups for the city and the state reveal close similarity in the percentage distribution among various age-groups. Two-fifth of the total population consists of infants and children falling within the age group of 0-14, about one-fifth population constitutes youths who are generally students in the age-group 15-24 years, while a large percentage of population lies within the age 25-50 years, because of employment in various government and semi-government organizations (Table 2). The percentage of males in the age-groups 15-24 years and 25-59 years is higher in

Dehradun as compared to urban areas of U.P. This is because of the predominance of college level students and workers of various offices and institutions.

Table 2
Distribution of Population According to Age-Groups and Sex-Composition in Dehradun City and U.P. (Urban) – 1981

Age Groups	*Dehradun City*			*Uttar Pradesh–Urban*		
(Years)	*Per cent*	*Per cent*	*Total*	*Percent*	*Per cent*	*Total*
0-14	19.8	20.4	40.2	21.6	19.5	41.1
15-24	11.3	8.4	19.7	10.7	8.1	18.8
25-59	21.2	14.3	35.3	19.8	14.8	34.6
60 & Above	2.9	1.9	4.8	3.3	2.2	5.5
Total			100.00			100.00

Table 3 presents age-group wise sex ratio in Dehradun and Uttar Pradesh urban. There is a decreasing trend in the sex ratio from 0-14 year's age-group to 60 years and above age group. The lower sex ratio in Dehradun might be due to working males living without their families and in-migration of male population in the age group of 25-59 years for seeking employment in Dehradun. The overall sex-ratio in Dehradun city is 852, according to 1981 census figures.

Table 3
Age Group wise Sex Ratio in Dehradun City and U.P. Urban–1981

Age Groups	*Dehradun City*			*Uttar Pradesh–Urban*		
(Years)	*Male*	*Female*	*Sex Ratio**	*Male*	*Female*	*Sex Ratio*
0-14	32,903	33,595	1,021	26,75,489	24,20,153	905
15-24	18,161	14,013	772	12,98,451	10,24,608	789
25-59	35,205	23,577	670	24,46,774	18,47,263	755
60 & Above	5,393	3,223	598	3,81,605	2,94,163	771

*Number of Female Per 1,000 Males.

As per 1981 census figures, Dehradun district has 52.02 per cent literarcy rate, which is highest in Uttar Pradesh which has a state average of 27.40 per cent. The percentage of literates in Dehradun city is 61.2 per cent which is 17.6 per cent higher than urban areas of U.P. The high rate of literacy in Dehradun city is also evident from the fact that the city claims to have highest per capita news paper consumption not only in the state but in the whole country. Table 4 presents the sex wise literacy rate in Dehradun city.

Table 4
Literacy Rate of Total Population–1981

Dehradun City		*Dehradun District*		*U.P. (Urban)*	
No. of Literates	*Percentage of Total*	*No. of Literates*	*Percentage of Total*	*No. of Literates*	*Percentage of Total*
1,01,671	61.2	1,69,432	62.3	54,04,708	43.6

Source for Tables 2, 3 and 4 – Master Plan for Dehradun – 1982-2001.

DEHRADUN: THE ETHNIC STRUCTURE

The presence of a large number of government organizations, research and educational institutions has attracted a good number of in migrants not only from the nearby areas but from all over the country also. These people from various cultural regions of the country have given Dehradun a cosmopolitan culture. Dehradun, though small in size represent a multi lingual, multi-ethnic and multi-religious society. These diverse ethnic groups have been living in perfect peace and harmony without any feeling of regionalism and ethnocentricism. They not only mix freely with each other but sometimes even to the extent of matrimonial alliances also.

When we talk about the urban social structure, the segregation and concentration of various group of population in different localities and enclaves is a universal phenomenon. In western class, structured societies, the higher income groups or upper classes are centralized in the middle of the city which is highly protected and provides maximum access to urban amenities, while the lower classes reside primarily in the perepheral zones which do not enjoy or command any urban civic amenities (Viswanadham, 1976). But recent researches have revealed a gradual break down of this traditional or 'colonial' pattern of residential segregation (Schner, 1967). This western economic model of residential segregation is not applicable in most of the Indian cities particularly in Dehradun. Here the residential segregation is primarily based on the place of origin, caste, religion, language and occupation.

For the purpose of present study the population of Dehradun may be classified into the following clearly distinguishable groups.

1.	Garhwalies	:	Local as well as migrated to and settled in Dehradun from other four districts of Garhwal region.
2.	Punjabis.	:	Migrated to Dehradun from Punjab (now Pakistan) in 1947 after partition. They may be sub-divided in two groups - (a) Sikhs and (b) non-Sikhs mainly Bannuwals.
3.	People from U.P. Plains		
4.	Bengalis	:	Came to Dehradun with Britishers as 'Kirani' and with the shifting of Survey of India from Calcutta to Dehradun.
5.	Christians		
6.	Gorkhas	:	Originally they came as invaders and latter on were brought by the Britishers with the establishment of Gorkha Regiment. Now permanently settled.
7.	Muslims		
8.	Scheduled Castes/ Backward Castes/ Scheduled tribes		
9.	Tibetans		

The map of Dehradun city shows a highly differentiated texture. Ethnic groups tend to cluster together in their own quarters. They may be distinguished from one another by language and culture. This living in close proximity or residential clustering is helpful in sustaining their sub-cultural values as it is possible only through the process of continuous interaction among people who share a common sub-culture (Bergal, 1955). Thus dominant cultural values become the fundamental principles of residential clustering and segregation. This is particularly true in case of immigrant population because they feel at home and comfortable when living in a locality belonging to their own regional culture.

Garhwalis or the people from the hill districts of Garhwal region constitute about thirty two per cent of city's popultion and is the largest single ethnic group irrespective of their caste affiliations. They are mainly engaged in services and petty trades. Dehradun being the largest town in entire Garhwal region, has attracted a large number of people from surrounding districts in search of jobs and better economic opportunities. These Garhwali people are found almost in every ward or locality but there are certain localities which are clearly predominantly inhabited by them. Ajabpur, Om Vihar, Dharampur, Vijay Colony, Arya Nagar and Chukhu Wala are clearly Garhwali dominated localities. The ongoing movement for a separate hill state has made this fact very much clear as most of the rallies and processions organized in favour of the movement mostly originate from these localities. Ajabpur-Dharampur situated on the eastern periphery of the city presents a picture of 'urban' surroundings rather than an urban area. This helps these people from rural areas of Garhwal to maintain and continue their rural and urban continuum. Garhwali clusters are also found around every big government office complex and are mostly occupied by the lower economic groups among them as the low paid persons serving in these organizations want to live in close proximity to their offices, to avoid the transportation costs.

The other prominent and clearly distinguishable group of population is Punjabis. Most of these Punjabis migrated to Dehradun from Punjab (Now Pakistan) in 1947, after the partition. The magnitude of Punjabi immigration to Dehradun can be assessed by comparing the population of city in 1941-51 decade which showed a decinal increase of 95.52 per cent. This is the second largest ethnic group in the population of Dehradun as they constitute about thirty per cent of the total population. This group can be broadly sub-divided into two groups–Sikhs who largely own the transportation and allied business, and Non-Sikh Punjabis constitute mainly Bannuwals and Sindhis. They are mainly engaged in trade and commerce. Both these groups are also found in the majority of wards of the city. They came to Dehradun as displaced persons so they were settled at two places mainly. First at Prem Nagar in the barracks, which were originally built for prisoners of war by the Britshers during World War I, and were lying unused after it (Lal, 1993). Secondly a substantial number of them occupied the houses deserted by the Muslims in Karanpur area. These two places still today represent the highest concentration of Punjabi population. The other localities which are identified as Punjabi dominated localities are Race Course, Govind Nagar (mostly inhabited by upper-middle class Sikhs). Ansari Road (mostly Sindhis), Patel Nagar, Laxman Chowk and Khurbura. The numerical dominance of Punjabis in Dehradun city is very clearly evident from the fact that in the last four general elections the city seat has been won three times by Punjabi candidates irrespective of their political affiliations.

Then come the number of groups of people from other districts of U.P. plains. The most dominant group among them is Vaish or Banias–the trader caste. They are among the earliest settlers and migrated to the city long back in 18th and 19th century from the neighbouring districts such as Saharanpur, Muzaffarnagar and Meerut. They have been the richest community monopolizing the wholesale trade and commerce. They mostly live in close proximity of trade and commercial centers of the city such as Paltan Bazar, Arhat Bazar, Raja Road, Anand Chowk, Chanda Mohalla, Dandipur and Tilak Road etc. As all these localities are situated in the heart of the city they are very congested consisting old 'Haveli' type buildings. Neo-rich among them have been shifting to more open and spacious upcoming new colonies on the periphery of the city.

Bengalis constitute an important ethnic group of Dehradun. They originally came to Dehradun in 19th century with the advent of British rule and the shifting of headquarters of 'Survey of India' from Calcutta to Dehradun. The Bengalis came here as 'Kiranis' or clerk and settled down here permanently (Lal, 1993). Now a days they occupy quite important positions as scientists and officers in Government organizations and research institutions, a few Bengali families are engaged in business. There is one locality in Dehradun known by the name of Bengali Mohalla and Bengali Library

Road which is indicative of their residential clustering in the bygone days. Now a days this locality is not dominated by Bengalis, but a large number of Bengali families have been living in close proximity to this area. This locality still has a 'Bangla Sahitya Samiti' and a commuity center exclusively used by Bengalis for their cultural and religious activities such as Durga Puja. It also houses a Bengali Library with a good collection of books and subscribe regularly to a number of Bengli magazines.

Christians form an important religious minority of Dehradun city. In the year 1859 a group of 40 Christians were brought by Mr.Wordside with him from Rohilkhand and were settled at Annfield agricultural colony belonging to the Church Mission in Derhadun (Williams, 1874). The predominance of Britishers in Dehradun in pre-independence days motivated a good amount of conversion into Christianity as it facilitiated the procurement of jobs as domestic help, cooks and butlers with the British families. At present numbering about 10,000 these Christians still live in the periphery of Rajpur Raod and Dalanwala once the exclusive localities developed by the Britishers for themselves. Nashvilla Road, Bakralwala and Dobhalwala have a very high percentage of Christians. Old Survey Road has an exclusive colony known by the name of Christian colony which has almost hundred per cent Christian population.

The Muslims, another religious minority in Dehradun, are not fractionated by caste but are quite explicitly stratified by class. Muslims constituting about 6.00 per cent of total population in Dehradun are the descendants of the early Muslim immigrants, the Sheikhs, Saiyads, Moughals and Pathans (Rohillas), and converts to Islam. Muslims first of all came here in 1757 with Najib-ud-doula, the Rohilla Nawab. Since then there has been a constant influx of Muslims to Dehradun city from the neighbouring districts of Saharanpur, Bijnore and Moradabad (U.P. district Gazetter, 1979). The lower classes among the Muslims mostly engaged as iron smiths, carpenters, barbers and petty fruit and vegetable merchants live in the tenanments of Innamulla Building on Gandhi Road and in a number of slums such as Muslim Colony behind Railway station, Idgah and the Muslim Colony situated at the crossing of Rajpur Road and Sahastradhara Road. In pre-indepenence period, Muslims enjoyed quite a good place in society as the whole Karanpur, now occupied by Punjabis, belonged to Muslims. This fact is evident from the presence of four mosques situated in the vicinity of Karanpur. The Muslim upper and middle class is not confined to any exclusive Muslim locality but they prefer to live in mixed localities.

Gorkhas (Nepalis) constitute an important ethnic and racial stock of Dehradun. Dehradun was invaded by Gorkhas in 1803 under the leadership Amar Singh Thapa and was annexed by them from Pradhyuman Sah, the Raja of Garhwal (Williams, 1874, Raturi, 1928). The Gorkhas remained in command of Dehradun till 1914, when Britishers drove them out and annexed Dehradun to Saharanpur district by a British government resolution, dated November 17, 1815. This is the cause of a number of Gorkha villages, such as Nehrugram, around Dehradun city. But the Gorkhas mainly clustered in Garhi, and Cantt. area settled here when the Britishers established the Headquarter of Gorkha Regiment at Dehradun and influenced by their bravery thereby extensive recruitement to it from Nepal during World War I.

Dehradun has quite a good number of backward castes, Scheduled castes and tribal population. As far as the backward castes are concerned, they mainly consist of Yadavs and Kurmis, who migrated to Dehradun in 19th century from central and eastern districts of U.P., to work as labourers with forest contractors and in tea gardens, have settled permanently in a number of villages after procuring land with their savings. Now they constitute the bulk of agricultural community around Dehradun. Some of them, who obtained education and have been able to procure one or the other urban occupation have settled down in the city area not in any specifically exclusive locality.

Scheduled castes in Dehradun mostly migrants from the surrounding districts of Saharanpur and Bijnore constitute the bulk of labour force in the city's trade and industry. Chamars outnumber all the scheduled castes as they constitute 42 per cent of the total scheduled caste population of the city. They came to Dehradun in the first half of 19th century to work in the lime industry, which was established and developed by them. In the beginning they were the owners of lime kilns. But later on the immigrant Punjabis entered into this business of lime and quarrying and with their business acumanship and enterpreneural abilities they captured the lime industry reducing the Chamars to the level of labourers in the industry, of which once they were the owners. Most of the Chamars along with other scheduled castes occupy the slum areas in the city. Almost all the 35 Malin Basties (slums) identified by M.D.D.A. and Municipal Board are predominantly inhabited by these scheduled castes and economically weaker sections mostly employed as labourers in industries and trade. These slums also represent a typical residential segregation based on caste and the place of origin e.g., Bijnori Chamars, mostly engaged in lime industries as labourers and in their traditional occupation, occupy the slums along the bank of river Rispna such as Ambedkar Colony, Nala Pani Road and Arya Nagar etc. The slums on the south-western side of Dehradun such as Indresh Colony and Rajiva Nagar are occupied by the scheduled caste people from eastern U.P. and Bihar. Most of these slums lie on the outskirts of the main city and totally lack urban amenties, such as severage or supply of soft drinking water.

Tibetans also constitute a sizeable number in the population of Dehradun. They came to Dehradun after the Chinese annexed Tibet. They came as refugees and were resettled in well defined and demarcated resettlement colonies at Rajpur, Sahasradhara Road and Clement Town. Being a very traditional and close society they generally do not interact socially or culturally with other cultural and ethnic groups in Dehradun.

The foregoing descriptions of various ethnic groups in Dehradun clearly indicate that these diverse groups generally follow the principles of residential segregation. The longing for emotional security and the desire to avoid hostile or unfriendly contacts contribute to the fostering of residential segregation (Bergel, 1995). Although the residential segregation of diverse ethnic groups reduces the number of actual conflicts but it aggravates the latent tensions among them by slowing the process of assimilation. By and large this segretative tendency is probably stronger among the uneducated and weaker classes than among families on the higher income and educational levels where caste or religious interests and loyalities, if they exist, become secondary, or even unimportant factors in selection of a resident (Gist, 1958).

As a result of rapid urban expansion and the development of better transport and coummunication facilities, new residential colonies have been developing very fast, generally on the outskirts of the city. This emergence of new residential areas mostly on the periphery has initiated a process of large scale centrifugal drift of population towards these new residential areas irrespective of caste, region and ethnic affiliations which has been ultimately destroying the traditionally prevalent residential segregation of ethnic groups not only in Dehradun but also in almost every large city in the country.

REFERENCES

Bergel, E.E. (1955), *Urban Sociology*, New York McGraw–Hill Book Company.

Bose, N.K. (1986), Calcutta: A Premature Matropolis, in *Readings in the urban Structure of India*, (eds.), G. Vishwanadham, New Delhi Ajanta Publications.

Ghosh, S. (1950), 'The Urban Papperna of Calcutta', *Economic Geography*, Vol. 26, January.

Gist, N.P. (1958), 'The Ecological Structure of an Asian City: An East-West Review', *Population Review*, Vol. 2, January.

Gupta, A. (1986), *'Doon Valley and Tourism'*, Unpublished M.A Dissertation, Garhwal University, Srinagar.

Govt. of U.P. (1979), U.P. District Gazetteers: Dehradun, Deptt. of District Gazetteers, Lucknow.

Govt. of U.P. (1985), *Master Plan for Dehradun*, 1982-2001, Town and Country Planning Department, Lucknow.

Lal, Prem H.H. (1993), *The Doon Valley Down the Ages*, New Delhi, Imprint.

Mehata, S.K. (1968), Patterns of Residence in Poona, India by Caste and Religion: 1922-1965, *Demography*, Vol. 6.

Mukherjee, Radha Kamal (1968), *Man and His Habitation* : A Study in Social Ecology, Bombay Popular Prakashan.

Scher, L.F. (1967), 'On the Spatial Structure of Cities in the Two Americas', in *The Study of Urbanization* (eds.) Phillip M. Hauser and L.F. Schnere, London, John Willey and Sons Inc..

Vishwanadham, G. (1976), *Urban Demography and Ecology*, New Delhi, Light and Life Publishers.

Vishwanadham, G. (1986), *Readings in the Urban Structure on India* (eds.) New Delhi Ajanta Publications.

Williams, G.R.C. (1974), (1985) *Memoirs of Dehradun*, Dehradun, Natraj Publishers.

Raturi, H.K. (1928), Garhwal Ka Itihas (Hindi), Dehradun.

4

FINGER DERMATOGLYPHICS VARIATION IN THE PASI COMMUNITY OF DEHRADUN (UTTAR PRADESH)

Bhakt R. Bhatnagar

The Pasi is a generic name referring to a score of populations notified as scheduled caste throughout the states of Uttar Pradesh, Bihar, West Bengal, Orissa, Punjab, Haryana, Himachal Pradesh and the union territories of Delhi, Chandigarh and some parts of Gujarat, Madhya Pradesh, Maharashtra and as far as South Karnataka.

The Pasi population in India, according to 1971 census, is 2,951,684 which is 0.54% of the total population of India. They constitute 3.69% and 21% of the total scheduled caste population of India and U.P. respectively. Out of the total Pasi population of India 94.95% live in villages, this is further increased to 97.40% at the state level. They are one of the15 most numerous scheduled caste of the country. In the state of U.P. they are mostly concentrated in a north-west, south-east belt running from the district of Kheri to Allahabad in the central plains with largest number in Sitapur, followed by Allahabad and Barabanki. They are sparsely distributed in the hills and plateau.

According to Crooke (1896), there are seven endogamous groups among the Pasi namely, the Raj, Gujar, Baurasi, Kaithwas, Arakh, Mothi and the 'Other Pasi'. While reviewing the earlier authors in this connection, Singh (1966) writes that "The Pasi community, which appears to be of a mixed origin, is related to the other groups and may be said to have an inner core group and a peripheral group. The core group would include Raj, Baurasi, Gujar, Kaithwas Pasi, Pasmagta and the peripheral group comprises of allied communities with which the Pasi have a strong affinity or a tradition of common origin or closer relationship in the past and the few may even now form their subcastes. This would include Arakh, Bhar, Khatick, Pachar, Mothi, and possibly Bahalie and Chiriyamar. Those in the core group are universally recognized as "Pasi".

It has been observed that the members of a Pasi subcaste generally marry among themselves and thus form a genetic isolate or a deme. The Pasi are occupationally toddy drawer, pig tamers, agriculturists, agricultural labourers and also employed as night watchman. There are very few Pasi employed in the government services.

Thus in the light of introduction of the Pasi community given above, it will be interesting to find out variations in terms of dermatoglyphic parameters, within the Pasi population and also to investigate trends of variation between Pasi population and populations of similar status in the neighbouring geographical proximity, on the one hand and on the other hand, with the populations of higher social status from whom they might have received genes while serving them. It may further be revealing to understand the effect of migration and subsequent isolation, in terms of dermatoglyphic traits.

MATERIAL AND METHOD

The data comprising of one hundred finger prints of individuals as far as possible unrelated from each of the four numerically dominant scheduled subcastes viz. Raj (RCUP), Baurasi (BCUP), Gujar (GCUP), and Kaithwas (KCUP) were collected in a door to door survey from Kheri, Sitapur, Barabanki, Lucknow, Raebareli and Pratapgarh districts of central U.P. This forms the parent population and members of three of those four subcastes namely, Baurasi (BDDN), Gujar (GDDN), and Kaithwas (KCUP), who migrated to Dehradun about three generations ago, as tea garden labourers, got settled there, form migrated population. In all 663 finger prints were collected following Cummins and Midlo (1961). They were also followed for identification scheme of finger print patterns.

The intra and inter population comparisons with respect to frequency of the whorl, loops, and arches have been done with the help of suitable statistical tests. The three co-ordinate graph projecting frequencies of whorls, loops and arches simultaneously, have been drawn to have a visual picture of all the U.P. population groups compared.

PRESENTATION AND INTERPRETATION

The distributions of finger patterns in the seven Pasi groups, hailing from two ecological zones of Uttar Pradesh, are given in Table 1. It may be observed from the table that the loops are relatively more than either whorls or the Arches in all the seven groups of the Pasi. The whorl percentage ranges from 36 to 48 while loops are 48 to 60% and aches show a frequency from 3 to 6%.

Table 1
Distribution of Finger Patterns in Seven Groups of the Pasi

Populations	*Locality*	*N*	*Three*	*Main*	*Types*
			Whorl	*Loop*	*Arch*
BDDN	Dehradun	100	36.5	60.0	2.6
GDDN	Dehradun	51	36.5	57.4	6.1
KDDN	Dehradun	112	40.6	53.8	5.6
BCUP	Lucknow & Rae Bareli	100	42.3	51.8	5.9
GCUP	Lucknow & Rae Bareli	100	37.7	56.9	5.4
KCUP	Rae Bareli & Pratapgarh	100	36.8	58.3	4.9
RCUP	Khri & Lucknow	100	47.8	48.4	3.8
All Pasi	Uttar Pradesh	663	40.0	55.2	4.8

A detailed analysis of Table 2 showing comparative bilateral distribution of pattern freqeuencies in the seven groups of the Pasi reveal that whorls range from 30.6% (KCUP) to 41.2% (RCUP) in the right hand and from 21.6 (GDDN) to

38.6% (RCUP), in the left hand, the range of variation is more in the Left hand in all the seven groups and maximum frequency in both the hands separately is found in RCUP group. The lateral pockets and twin loops have a range of 2.2% (BDDN) to 5.1% (GDDN) in the right hand and from 4.2% (BDDN) to 8.4% (BCUP). Here again the range of variation in the left hand is more as compared to the right hand and minimum frequency is found among BDDN in both the hands individually. Except RCUP where the frequency of these two configurations is equal, it is always more on the left hand as compared to the right in remaining six groups. The incidence of central pockets loops ranges from 1% (KCUP) to 2.6% (RCUP) in the right hand, whereas it varies from 1.6% (BCUP) to 3.1% (GDDN), again the range is more in the left hand.

Accindental configuration is rare, always less than 1%. It is further observed from the same table that the frequency of radial loops ranges from 1.6% (GDDN) to 5.2% (RCUP) in the corresponding right hands of all the seven groups and in the left hand it is found that ulnar loops are more as compared to radial loops, frequency of which ranges from 42.2% (RCUP) to 57.6% (BCUP) in the right hand and from 44.2% (RCUP) to 60.0% (GDDN) in the left hand. Combined (R+L) frequency of Ulnar Loops is maximum in BDDN (58.6%) and minimum in RCUP group (43.2%). Tented Aches are found to vary from 0.6% (BDDN) to 2.6% (BCUP) in the right hand from 0.01% (BCUP) to 2.8% (KCUP). Total percentage of Arches vary from 1.8% (BDDN) to 6.7% (GDDN).Thus Loops are maximum in frequency followed by Whorls and Arches in descending order. Pooled frequencies of all the Pasi groups together show the same trends.

To see the bilateral difference in the frequency of finger patterns the pooled frequency of all the digits in the right and left hand is subjected to Chi square test in each group. It is interesting to note that bilateral Chi-square values in all the seven groups are not significant (Table 2), therefore the pooled (R+L) frequencies in each of the group is presented in the last row.

Table 2
Bilateral Distribution of Pattern Frequencies in the Seven Groups of the Pasi from Uttar Pradesh

Pasi		*WHORLS*					*LOOPS*			*ARCHES*				
Groups	*Side*	*True Whorls*	*Lateral pockets & Twin Loops*	*Central pocket*	*Accidentals*	*Total*	*Rdl.*	*Ulr.*	*Total*	*Tented*	*Others*	*Total*	*Bilateral*	*Chi-Square Valves*
Buarasi	R	31.0	2.2	1.8	0.2	38.2	2.4	57.6	60.0	0.6	1.2	1.8	3.384	ns
	L	27.4	4.2	2.6	0.6	34.8	2.2	59.6	61.8	1.4	1.0	3.4		
Dehradun	R+L	30.7	3.2	3.2	0.4	36.5	2.3	58.6	60.9	1.0	1.6	2.6		
Gujar	R	34.1	5.1	1.6	0.4	41.2	1.6	51.7	53.3	0.8	4.7	5.5	4.907	ns
	L	21.6	7.1	3.1	0.0	31.8	1.6	60.6	61.6	2.0	4.7	6.7		
Dehradun	R+L	27.8	6.1	2.4	0.2	36.5	1.6	55.9	57.4	1.4	4.7	6.1		
Kaithwes	R	37.7	2.7	2.1	0.2	42.7	1.9	49.3	51.1	1.4	4.8	6.2	5.622	ns
	L	30.7	5.4	2.0	0.4	38.4	2.7	53.9	56.6	1.2	3.8	5.0		
Dehradun	R+L	34.2	4.0	2.0	0.3	40.5	2.2	51.6	53.8	1.3	4.3	5.6		
Baurasi Central U.P.	R	34.8	4.8	2.0	0.0	41.6	2.4	50.4	52.8	2.6	3.0	5.6	0.387	ns
	L	32.8	8.4	1.6	0.2	46.0	1.4	49.4	50.8	0.01.	4.8	6.2		
	R+L	33.8	6.6	1.8	0.1	42.3	1.9	49.9	51.8	0.0	3.2	5.9		
Gujar Central U.P.	R	31.6	3.0	2.6	0.0	37.8	3.0	53.2	56.2	1.6	4.4	6.0	0.686	ns
	L	29.0	5.6	2.4	0.6	37.6	2.4	55.2	57.6	1.8	3.0	4.8		
	R+L	30.0	4.6	2.5	0.3	37.7	2.7	54.5	56.9	1.7	3.7	5.4		

Contd...

Pasi				WHORLS				LOOPS			ARCHES			
Groups	Side	True Whorls	Lateral pockets & Twin Loops	Central pocket	Accidentals	Total	Rdl.	Ulr.	Total	Tented	Others	Total	Bilateral	Chi-Square Valves
Kaithwas	R	30.6	4.6	1.0	0.4	36.6	1.6	57.2	58.8	2.2	2.4	4.6	0.265	ns
Central	L	27.4	5.6	3.4	0.6	37.9	2.8	55.0	57.8	2.8	2.4	5.2		
U.P.	R+L	20.9	5.1	2.2	0.5	36.8	2.2	56.1	58.3	2.5	2.4	4.9		
Raj	R	41.2	5.0	2.6	0.4	49.2	5.2	42.2	47.4	1.8	1.6	3.4	1.025	ns
Central	L	38.6	5.0	2.8	0.0	46.4	5.2	44.2	49.4	2.6	1.6	4.2		
U.P.	R+L	39.9	5.0	2.7	0.2	47.8	5.2	43.2	48.4	2.2	1.6	3.8		
All Pasi	R	35.0	3.9	2.0	0.2	41.1	2.6	51.1	54.2	1.6	3.1	4.7		
Pooled	L	30.3	5.8	2.5	0.4	38.9	2.7	53.4	56.1	1.9	3.1	5.0		
	R+L	32.6	4.8	2.3	0.3	40.0	2.6	37.4	55.2	1.5	3.1	4.8		

INTRA POPULATION COMPARISONS

The intra population comparisons with respect to pattern frequencies (Table 3) reveal that all the seven groups are not homogeneous for this trait. Most variable are the BDDN and RCUP groups which show significant differences in all the six pairs of comparisons whereas, GDDN and KDDN groups are significantly different in two pair of comparisons each, whereas BCUP, GCUP and KCUP groups show significant differences in the pair of comparisons each.

The RCUP is significantly different because of maximum frequency of total Whorls and minimum frequency of total Loops, whereas BDDN is significantly different, because of maximum frequency of total Loops and minimum frequency of total Whorls.

The comparisons between parent and migrant group pairs namely GCUP-GDDN and KCUP-KDDN do not significantly differ either on the basis of Pattern types chi-square, A/W proportions or PI Index. Only BCUP-BDDN differs significantly because of more Whorls and Arches and comparatively less Loops in the former than the latter group.

Singh (1966), while studying finger patterns of the Pasi hand, has outlined "The chief characteristic feature of the Pasi hand, to be very high frequency of Radial Loops in the left II digit and the bimannual difference of an extreme type in this trait". He further adds that "this high value of 22.45% is unsurpassed by any of the series from U.P. till date". The above observation is supported by the parent data upto the extent that combined (R+L) frequency Loops in the II digit is maximum as compared to the other digits but it is variable between left and right II digits. The second observation of Singh showing 22.45% Radial Loops on the Left II digit is still unsurpassed by any of the present Pasi groups. Singh has further quoted Mujumdar's observation that "High B and low O resemble with criminal tribes of U.P. but there is no material evidence to prove that like other vagarant criminal tribes of U.P., The Pasis have also canalized alien blood into the veins of the tribe on a large scale through the compromising morals

Table 3
Homogeniety Chi-square within Pasi Groups and Between Pasi and other Populations from Uttar Pradesh

Populations Compared	*BDDN*	*GDDN*	*KDDN*	*BCUP*	*GCUP*	*KCUP*	*RCUP*
Rajputs	22.68*	11.14*	6.12*	6.39*	12.53*	16.00*	1.38
Ahirs	6.07*	11.62*	11.14*	16.13*	9.54*	10.71*	15.38*
Purabia Chamar	21.97*	2.41	10.93*	10.78*	7.63*	7.02*	37.27*
Gujar Pasi (S&S)	7.02	0.18	1.57	2.60	0.42	0.26	14.15*
Brahman Kanyakubja	5.42	8.47*	7.34*	11.61*	6.15*	7.53*	12.96*
Brahman Saryuparin	16.30*	1.24	0.55	0.94	2.22	3.57	14.91*
Restogis	30.73*	6.28*	2.22	0.31	9.75*	12.82*	10.10*
Gujar Pasi (T&P)	1.44	3.30	9.49*	14.42*	2.46	1.46	30.34*
KureelChamar	2.74	2.75	5.22	9.22*	1.32	1.20	20.93*
Pasi (Rae Bareli)	1.80	6.85*	9.17*	13.97*	4.61	4.66	20.21*
Muslims	40.90*	25.77*	20.70*	19.55*	31.00*	36.01*	2.02
Muslim Sayyad	5.47	12.53*	13.21*	19.45*	10.09*	11.42*	19.27*
Muslim Pathan	54.36*	39.80*	34.75*	32.05*	46.47*	51.33*	10.82*
Khatri (EUP)	0.46	5.86	10.72*	14.61*	3.83	4.44	23.10*
Khatri (CUP)	2.74	8.31*	8.25*	11.73*	6.32*	6.32*	12.76*
BDDN	-	11.32*	18.45*	24.50*	11.39*	7.69*	31.76*
GDDN		-	2.36	4.98	0.55	1.06	19.18*
KDDN			-	0.91	1.98	4.22	12.96*
BCUP				-	5.25	8.68*	9.15*
GCUP					-	0.41	21.62*
KCUP						-	24.91*

* Values significant at 5% level.

of their women". In this connection it is indicated in the present findings that the two groups namely, BCUP and GCUP show higher percentage of B gene as compared to O gene but the other two groups namely KCUP and RCUP exhibit higher percentage of A gene than B (Bhatnagar, 1973). It is interesting to point out that an increase in B phenotype is associated with corresponding increase in Arch/Whorl index value in all the four groups studied from central Uttar Pradesh.

The pattern frequencies of seven Pasi groups under study have been projected on a three co-ordinate graph which shows RCUP to be different (Figure 1) from rest of the six groups. It is Arch axis which divides U.P. Pasi groups into two clusters one is formed by RCUP on one side and the other six Pasi groups on other side.

The mean PI Index in the seven Pasi groups (Table 4) varies from 13.2 (GDDN) to 14.6 (RCUP). It may be noted that RCUP group significantly differs with remaining five Pasi groups, except BCUP which is inseparable in this character (Table 5). The RCUP and BCUP, being close to each other in the frequency of Whorl and Loop do not show significant difference. All other Pasi group pairs do not significantly differ with their partners.

The Arch/Whorl or Dankmeijer Index (Table 4) varies from 7.1 (BDDN) to 16.7 (GDDN). The BDDN group is close to RCUP in this trait than rest of the five groups. This index is found to be most distinguishing character. The standard error of difference calculated between proportions of Arch/Whorl between all the Pasi group pairs show that RCUP group does not significantly differ with BDDN and BCUP groups, therefore, significant difference in pattern types shown by these two pairs is because of differences in the Loop frequency. Same is the case with BCUP-KCUP pair. All other remaining 9 pair of comparisons (Table 3) do not show significant differences between pattern types as well as A/W proportions.

The Whorl/Loop or Furuhata Index (Table 4) shows a reverse trend than that shown by Arch/Whorl Index. The BDDN group shows maximum (98.8) mean value for this Index. The range of variation over seven groups for both the index is considerable. Furuhata Index however, splits the seven groups into two segments and is presented by BDDN, GDDN, KCUP and the other by KDDN, BCUP, GCUP, RCUP groups.

INTER POPULATION COMPARISONS

The percentage frequencies of Whorls, Loops and Arches in fifteen comparable groups from Uttar Pradesh are listed in Table 5. It is clear from the Table that all the populations show higher frequency of Loops than Whorls or Arches. Only Muslim samples are exception.All these groups are compared with seven population groups of the Pasi by 2 × 3 contingancy table and the results are presented in Table 6. All but two groups show significant differences with RCUP group, they are Rajputs and Muslims. It may be noted here that RCUP group shows dissimilarities with other Pasi groups but similarities with Rajputs and Muslims for this character. It is further interesting to note that other three Pasi groups namely BCUP, GCUP and KCUP show dissimilarities with other caste groups claiming higher caste origin such as Rajputs, Ahirs, and Khatri (CUP) on one hand and with Muslims and Chamars on the other. Only Saryuparin Brahmans are exception to the above statement. The Gujar Pasi (S&S) group is however similar to the three groups namely BCUP, GCUP and KCUP. It is also observed that GCUP and KCUP groups cannot be separated from Gujjar Pasi (T&P), Kureel Chamar, Pasi (Raebareli) and Khatri (EUP), whereas BCUP group shows significant differences with these groups for this character. The Rastogi sample from Lucknow shows reverse trend i.e., they are closer to BCUP then rest of the three groups. When all these groups are compared with three Pasi samples from Dehradun an overlapping picture is obtained. Ahirs and Muslims are close to the sample of Kureel Chamars as revealed by the Chi-square results. An indepth analysis of the Chi-square results show that BDDN group does not show significant differences with Kanyakubja Brahmans, Gujar Pasi (T&P), Pasi Raebarali, Muslim (Sayyad), Khatri (EUP) and Khatri (CUP) whereas they are significantly different from Purabia Chamars,Gujjar Pasi (S&S), Brahman Saryuparin, Rastogis, Muslims and Pathan

Table 4

Distribution of Pattern Intensity, Denkmeijer and Furuhata Indices in the Pasi and other Populations from Uttar Pradesh

Population Groups	*N*	*PII*	*S.E.*	*Dankmeijer Index*	*Furuhata Index*	*Investigator*
Rajputs	103	1.16		9.11	91.27	Singh, 1961
Ahirs	114	13.85		7.05	74.33	Singh, 1961
Purabia Chamar	75	12.67	±0.49	23.08	60.40	Srivastava *et al.*, 1966
Gujar Pasi (S&S)	55	13.58	±0.42	14.28	67.74	Srivastava *et. al.*, 1966
Kanyabkubja Brahman	100	13.76	±0.34	7.26	72.82	Shukla, *et al.*, 1969
Saryuparin Brahmin	100	13.26	±0.41	17.95	76.09	Shukla *et al.*, 1969
Rastogis	150	13.62		13.40	88.36	Rastogi, 1972
Gujar Pasi (T&P)	100	13.24	±0.89	12.74	72.64	Tandon & Pandey, 1975
Kureel Chamar	100	13.22	±0.92	12.03	73.11	Tandon & Pandey, 1975
Pasi (Rbi)	98	13.55		7.25	69.43	Singh, 1966
Muslims	100	14.67		6.00	106.38	Singh, 1961
BDDN	100	13.50	±0.31	7.12	59.93	Bhatnagar, Present Study
GDDN	51	13.24	±0.53	16.67	63.48	Bhatnagar, Present Study
KDDN	112	13.55	±0.36	13.97	74.35	Bhatnagar, Present Study
BCUP	100	13.81	±0.37	13.95	81.66	Bhatnagar, Present Study
GCUP	100	13.35	±0.37	14.36	66.08	Bhatnagar, Present Study
KCUP	100	13.41	±0.30	13.9	62.78	Bhatnagar, Present Study
RCUP	100	14.63	±0.33	7.95	98.76	Bhatnagar, Present Study
Muslim Sayyads	150	13.81	±0.27	6.85	72.55	Shukla & Srivastava, 1969a
Muslim Pathan	50	15.34	±0.53			Srivastavam 1972
Khatri (CUP)	45	13.60	±0.50			Tyagi, 1973
Khatri (EUP)	35	13.20	±0.60			Tyagi, 1973

Table 5

Distribution (Percentage) of Finger Pattern Types in Population of Uttar Pradesh

Populations	*Locality*	*N*	*Sex*	*Three Whorl*	*Main Loop*	*Patterns Arch*	*Investigator*
Rajputs	U.P.	103	M	45.70	50.1	4.2	Singh, 1961
Ahirs	U.P.	100	M	41.1	55.7	2.9	Singh, 1961
Muslims	U.P.	100	M	49.9	46.9	3.2	Singh, 1961
Purabia Chamaars	Hardoi	75	M	35.0	56.7	7.9	Srivastava & Shukla, 1966
Gujar Pasi	Lucknow	55	M	38.7	56.7	4.6	Srivastava & Shukla, 1966
Kanykubja Brahmans	Lucknow	100	M	41.3	55.7	3.0	Shukla & Srivastava, 1969
Saryuparin	Lucknow	100	M	40.1	52.7	6.1	Shukla & Srivastava, 1969
Rastogis	Lucknow	150	M	43.5	50.6	5.9	Rastogi, 1972
Gujar Pasi	Lucknow	100	M	36.3	59.9	4.1	Tandon & Pandey, 1975
Kureel Chamar	Lucknow	100	M	37.5	58.4	4.1	Tandon & Pandey, 1975
Pasi	Raebareli	98	M	39.4	57.8	2.9	Singh, 1966
Khatri	Eastern U.P.	35	M	34.8	62.0	3.1	Tyagi, 1973
Khatri	Central U.P.	45	M	40.2	56.7	3.1	Tyagi, 1973
Sayyad Muslims	Lucknow	150	M	40.9	56.3	2.6	Srivastava & Shukla 1969a
Pathan Muslims	Lucknow	50	M	55.6	42.2	2.2	Srivastava, 1972

Table 6
Values of 't' Test for PII between Pasi and other Populations from Uttar Pradesh

Population Groups	*GDDN*	*KDDN*	*BCUP*	*GCUP*	*KCUP*	*RCUP*	*GP (T&P)*	*Ku. CHA*	*GP (S&S)*	*PU Cha*	*Ashraf Muslim*
BDDN	.484	.211	1.024	.207	.229	2.43*	.273	.188	.139	1.445	1.310
GDDN	-	.976	1.406	.308	.325	2.233*	.038	.114	.527	.736	1.384
LDDM		-	.387	.392	.427	2.071*	.373	.288	.033	1.554	.957
BCUP			-	.762	.828	1.608	.575	.490	.424	1.852	.372
GCUP				-	.021	2.441*	.165	.082	.297	1.206	1.412
KCUP					-	2.684*	.169	.084	.315	1.281	1.618
RCUP						-	1.423	1.332	1.749	3.316*	1.592
Gujar Pasi (T&P)							-	.063	.334	.559	.811
Kureel Chamar								-	.254	.254	.720
Gujar Pasi (S&S)									-	1.335	.774
Purabia Chamar										-	2.496*
Ashraf Muslim											-

Muslims. Similarly GDDN and KDDN samples differ significantly from Kanyakubja Brahmans, Pasi (Rb), Muslim Sayyad, Muslim Pathan, and Khatri (CUP) but are indistinguishable from Gujjar Pasi (S&S) and Saryuparin Brahmans for this character. In addition to the above mentioned samples KDDN sample differs significantly with Purabia Chamars, Gujar Pasi (T&P) and Khatri (EUP) while GDDN group shows similarity with these groups.

The three co-ordinate graph does not reveal much information with respect to distribution of fifteen U.P. populations except that all the groups are closely gathered around Arch axis. This is because of less frequency of Arches in all the U.P. populations as compared to frequencies of either Whorls or Loops.

Arch/Whorl Index (Table 4) varies from Muslims (6.00) to Purabia Chamars (23.08) in 22 U.P. populations including seven Pasi groups. On screening of these values it is revealed that

Populations	*W*	*L*	*A*
BDDN	36.5	60	2.6
GDDN	36.5	57.4	6.1
KDDN	40.6	53.8	5.6
BCUP	42.3	51.8	5.9
GCUP	37.7	56.9	5.4
KCUP	36.8	58.3	4.9
RCUP	47.8	48.4	3.8
All Pasi	40	55.2	4.8
Rajputs	45.7	50.1	4.2
Ahirs	41.1	55.7	2.9
Muslims	49.9	46.9	3.2
Purabia Chamaars	35	56.7	7.9
Gujar Pasi	38.7	56.7	4.6
Kanykubja Brahmans	41.3	55.7	3
Saryuparin	40.1	52.7	6.1
Rastogis	43.5	50.6	5.9
Gujar Pasi	36.3	59.9	4.1
Kureel Chamar	37.5	58.4	4.1
Pasi	39.4	57.8	2.9
Khatri	34.8	62	3.1
Khatri	40.2	56.7	3.1
Sayyad Muslims	40.9	56.3	2.6
Pathan Muslims	55.6	42.2	2.2

most of the populations show this value to more than 10.0 excepting Muslims, Rajputs, Ahirs, Kanyakubja Brahmans, Pasi (Rb), BDDN and RCUP.

Whorl/Loop Index (Table 4) on the other hand ranges from 60.46 (Purabia Chamars) to 106.38 (Muslims). More than average value is found among Rajputs, Rastogies, Muslims and RCUP groups. All other groups have shown less than average value of this Index.

Only five populations groups from U.P. could be compared (Table 5) with seven Pasi groups with respect to PI Index because of non availability of standard deviations in the studies reported. It is interesting to note that all the Pasi groups compared with Gujjar Pasi (T&P), Kureel Chamars, Gujar Pasi (S&S), Purabia Chamar and Ashraf Muslim do not show significant differences with each other excepting Purabia Chamars who are significantly different from RCUP and Ashraf Muslim samples.

ACKNOWLEDGEMENT

I am grateful to Dr. R.K. Bhattacharya, Director, Anthropological Survey of India, for providing necessary working facilities. I am also thankful to Shri R.B. Bhale for statistical calculations and to all those Pasi subjects for their co-operation without which it would have been impossible to complete this project.

REFERENCES

Bhatnagar, B.R. (1973), ABO, Blood Groups among the Pasi: A Scheduled Caste of Uttar Pradesh, *J. Indian Anthrop. Soc.* 8 : 173-177.

Bhatnagar, B.R. (1974), Mannus Middle Phalangeal Hair Variability among the Pasi, *The Eastern Anthropologist*, 27: 205-210.

Census of India (1971), Special Volume on Scheduled Castes and Scheduled Tribes.

Crook, W. (1896), *The Castes and Tribes of N W Provinces and Oudh.* Vol. IV: 138-152, Calcutta.

Rastogi, S., P.K. Tiwari and D. Tyagi (1977), Finger Dermatoglyphics of the Rastogis of Lucknow. Proc. 3rd Conf. of E.F.C.S. and I.A.P.A. Lucknow (U.P.).

Shukla, B.R.K. and A.C. Srivastava (1969a), Finger Dermatoglyphic Study of the Pathans of Malihabad, Lucknow (U.P.).

Shukla, B.R.K. and R.P. Srivastava (1969b), A Quantitative Finger Dermatoglyphics of the Brahmans of Uttar Pradesh, *J. Ind. Anthrop. Soc.* 4 : 165-173.

Singh, H.N. (1972), Census of India 1971,Series I–India Monograph Series Part V. Pasi (A Scheduled Caste in Uttar Pradesh).

Singh, R.D. (1961), Digital Pattern Frequency and Size Variation in some Castes of Uttar Pradesh, *The Eastern Anthroplogist*, 14 : 169-181.

Srivastava, A.C. (1972), The Finger Prints of Sayyads of Lucknow, U.P. *Acta. Genet. Med. Gem.* 21: 337-349.

Srivastava, R.P. and Shukla, B.R.K. (1966), A Quantitative Study of Dermatoglyphics of Purabia Chamars and Gujar Pasi of Uttar Pradesh, *The Anthropologist* 13: 65-71.

Tandon, V.K. and Nisha Pandey (1975), Inter Population Distance in Finger Dermatoglyphics: A Study based on Gujar Pasi and Kureel Chamar, *I.J.P.A. and H.G.* 1: 153-161.

Tyagi, D. (1973), Dermatoglyphics of Khatri of U.P. – An unpublished Report.

5

DIFFERENTIAL FERTILITY OF THE GARHWALIS OF DEHRADUN

Swapna Chowdhury

In the city of Dehradun, since a considerable time, a fairly large number of Garhwalis were settled. Most of them originally belong to the district of Tehri Garhwal and Pauri Garhwal. They have mostly adopted different kinds of non-traditional occupation for their subsistence. The study focuses itself on the dynamics of Garhwali fertility in an urban setting of Dehradun. For this purpose two major caste groups of Garhwali population, namely, the Brahman and the Rajput were selected.

The present paper attempts initially, to describe the fertility trend and differentials among the two Garhwali populations and then to ascertain the variation in bio-events and family planning practices.

MATERIAL AND METHODS

Demographic data were collected from 127 households of Garhrwali Brahman and 72 households of Garhwali Rajput, living in Dehradun city. Fertility information was collected by geneological method from living ever married women. In addition to this, information on family planning practices and bio-events of married women were also recorded.

RESULTS AND DISCUSSION

From age, sex and marital status composition of two populations shown in Table 1, it appears that 42.4%, 47.8% and 9.8% in Garhwal Brahman, and 39.7%, 52.05% and 8.2% in Garhwali Rajput, are in the age groups of 0-14, 15-49 and 50+ years respectively, a distribution which suggests relatively greater growth potential of the former group. When the four main age groups : 0-4, 5-14, 15-49 and 50+, are compared following Gupta (1980), the apparent difference between the two Garhwali populations in age and sex structure is found insignificant (t 0.18, df 7, p>0.05).Unlike typically growing populations, the base of the pyramids (0-4 years age group) are not the broadest (Figure 1), suggesting a recent fertility decline in the absence of any cause of death, largely involving the infants.The sex ratio (the number of females per 1000 males) among the Garhwali Brahman (982) and the Garhwali Rajput (900) shows preponderence of males over females. The child woman ratio, defined as the number of children under 5 years of age per 100 women aged 15-45 years, is 55.63 and 54.54 in the Garhwali Brahman and Rajput, respectively, suggests higher fertility in the former than the latter group (Table 1).

Table 2 exhibits the average number of live births and survival of children per mother which are 4.0 and 3.5 respectively, in the Garhwali Brahman and 3.5 and 3.0 respectively, in the Garhwali Rajput population. The difference between the two groups with respect to survival of children is found significant at 5 per cent level (t 2.57, df 209, p>0.05).

Table 3 shows the distribution of mothers in both the populations according to live births in different age groups; 25-29, 30-34, 35-39, 40-44, 45 years and above who are in continuous wedlock. The statistical analysis failed to indicate any significant difference between the two groups in respect of distribution of mother according to live births. From the fertility performance of the Garhwali women aged 45 years and above, we find that the completed family size is 5.6 in the Garhwali Brahman and 4.9 in the Garhwali Rajput, the difference between them is, however, insignificant.

Table 1
Age, Sex and Married Status of Garhwali Brahman and Garhwali Rajput

Population	Age Groups (Years)	Unmarried		Married		WDS*		Total				Sex Ratio	Child Women
		Male	Female	Male	Female	Male	Female	Male No.	Female No.	Male+Female No.	%		
Garhwali	0-14	141	148					141	148	289	42.37	1048	
Brahman	15-49	60	44	99	122		1	159	167	326	47.80	1050	
	50+			43	19	1	4	44	23	67	9.82	522	
	Total	101	87	142	141	1	5	344	338	682		982	55.63
Garhwali	0-14	78	67					78	67	145	39.73	858	
Rajput	15-49	39	22	58	71			97	93	190	52.05	969	
	50+			16	6	1	7	17	13	30	8.22	678	
	Total	117	89	74	77	1	7	192	173	365		900	54.54

*Widow/Divorced/Separated

Figure-1: ***Age Pyramids of Two Garhwali Population***

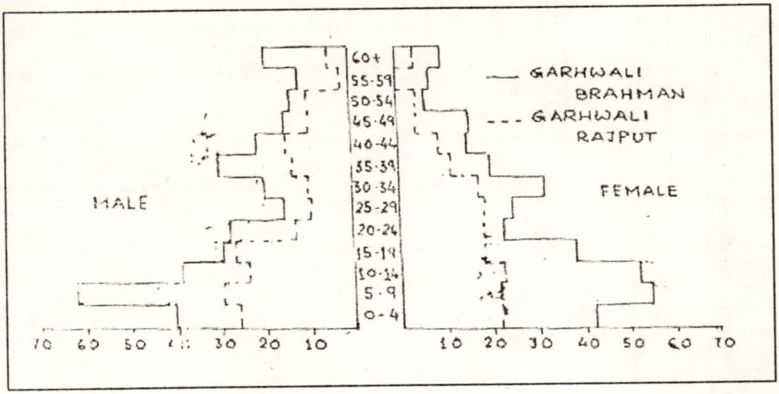

Table 2
Number of Married Women by Surviving and Total Sibship Size

No. of Surviving Children	*Garhwali Brahman*		*Garhwali Rajput*		*No. of Live Births*	*Garhwali Brahman*		*Garhwali Rajput*	
	No.	%	No.	%		No.	%	No.	%
0	1	0.7	3	3.9	0	1	0.7	2	2.6
1	13	9.6	8	10.5	1	10	7.4	8	10.5
2	21	15.6	20	26.3	2	20	14.8	11	14.5
3	40	29.6	17	22.4	3	34	25.2	19	25.0
4	26	19.3	14	22.4	4	23	17.0	15	19.7
5	17	12.6	8	10.5	5	19	14.1	13	17.1
6	7	5.2	2	2.6	6	10	7.4	3	4.0
7	8	5.9	1	1.3	7	12	8.9	4	5.3
8	2	1.5			8	5	3.7	1	1.3
9					9	0			
10					10	0			
11					11	1	0.7		
Total	135		76		Total	135		76	
Mean No. per female	3.5		3.0		Total	4.0		3.5	

t = 2.57, d.f. 209, P<0.05t = 1.76, d.f. = 209, P<0.05

Table 3

No. of Live Births by Age Groups of Married Women Living in Wedlock

Married Women having live	Frequency of married women by age groups									
	25-29 years		30-34 years		35-39 years		40-44 years		45 and above	
	Garhwali Brahman	Garhwali Rajput	Garhwali Brahman	Garhwali Rajput	Garhwali Brahman	Garhwali Rajput	Garhwali Brahman	Garhwali Rajput	Garhwali Brahman	Garhwali Rajput
0	1	1								
1	1	3	1							
2	6	2	5	2	2	2	1		1	1
3	7	8	14	4	6	4	3	1	4	1
4	5	2	7	7	3	2	3	3	5	1
5	1	0	3	3	5	3	5	3	5	4
6					2		1	2	7	3
7			1		3		1	1	7	1
8					1	1	1		3	
9										
10										
11									1	
Total	21	16	31	16	22	12	15	10	33	11
Mean	2.8	2.4	3.2	3.7	4.5	3.9	4.6	4.9	5.6*	4.9*
S.D.	1.17	1.15	1.29	0.95	1.74	1.68	1.59	1.20	1.90	1.45

t = 0.97, df = 35, P>0.05t = 1, df = 45, P>0.05t = 1.03, df = 32, P>0.05t = 0.54, df = 23, P>0.05t = 1.27, df = 42, P>0.05

The total fertility rate of women living in the wedlock is higher among the Garhwali Brahman (4.0) than among the Garhwali Rajput (3.5) (Table 4). The age specific fertility among the married women now aged 45 + years in the Garhwali Rajput is generally lower than in the Brahman. Considering the females of all ages it appears that the fertility in the two younger age groups, i.e., below 25 and 25-34 years, is almost similar in the two populations but thereafter the Garhwali Brahman group exhibits higher rates.

Table 4
Live Births during each 5 Years Period to Married Women Living in Wedlock by Percentage

Age period (Years)	*Present age of married women (Years)*									
	< 25		*25-34*		*35-44*		*45+*		*All ages*	
	GB (13)*	*GR** (11)*	*GB* (52)*	*GR** (32)*	*GB* (37)*	*GR** (22)*	*GB* (33)*	*GR** (11)*	*GB* (133)*	*GR** (76)*
< 19	0.31	0.36	0.33	0.44	0.41	0.68	0.45	0.54	0.38	0.51
20-24	1.08	1.27	1.44	1.41	1.57	1.86	1.61	1.54	1.48	1.54
25-29			1.00	1.06	1.51	1.09	1.55	1.45	1.18	0.97
30-34			0.35	0.16	0.86	0.54	1.24	1.09	0.67	0.38
35-39					0.19	0.18	0.64	0.27	0.21	0.09
40-44					0.03		0.12		0.04	
45+										
Total fertility rate							5.61	4.91	4.00	3.50

No. of Women in Parentheses.
*Garhwali Brahman; **Garhwali Rajput

BIO-EVENT

Table 5 shows some bio-events of the Garhwali women of two different caste groups along with their mean adolescent sterility period. Only in respect of menarcheal age, significant difference was observed between the two Garhwali populations ($t = 2.40$, $df = 224$, $p>0.05$). However, women of the present Garhwali populations offer higher values of mean menarcheal age (above 16 years) as compared to the earlier reported mean menarcheal age of Hindu women (13.6 ± 0.07 years) of Uttar Pradesh

(Dubey and Srivastava, 1965) and Punjabi Khatris (13.9 ± 0.08 years) and Sindhis (13.8 ± 0.07 years) of Delhi (Ghosh and Kumar, 1973).

Table 5
Bio-Events and Adult Sterility Period

Age at	*Garhwali Brahman*				*Garhwali Rajput*			
(in Years)	*N*	*Mean*	*SD*	*Range*	*N*	*Mean*	*SD*	*Range*
Marriage	141	17.1	2.76	10-25	85	17.0	2.96	09-26
Menarche	141	16.6	1.88	13-24	85	16.1	1.47	13.-19
First child birth	136	20.5	2.59	15-29	82	20.2	2.55	15-27
Menopause	22	45.2	3.59	39-50	12	46.4	3.85	40-52
Adolescent Sterility	137	2.3	1.64	Below 1-10 years	82	2.5	1.79	Below 1-10 years

FAMILY PLANNING PRACTICES

Both the Garhwali populations have greatly accepted the family planning practices, the adoption rate being more than 54% (Table 6). More tubectomy and vasectomy cases are reported by the Garhwali Rajput couples than the Garhwali Bahman couples. Married women of 25-34 years of age groups in the Garhwali Rajput population show more adoption of family planning practices than the Garhwali Brahman but in the immediate progressive age group, i.e. 35-44 years, trend is just opposite.

Finally we may conclude that no statistically significant difference between the Garhwali Brahman and Rajput populations, settled in Dehradun city, are detectable with regard to age and sex structure and fertility except in case of average number of surviving children to women of all ages, probably owing to sharing of similar socio-economic environment. A very high rate of adoption of family planning methods and higher mean menarcheal age of women of these Garhwali groups as compared to the neighbouring populations of Uttar Pradesh and Delhi, are the two distinct features which are known to have their impacts on fertility.

Table 6
Family Planning Practices by Age Group of Married Women*

Age Group of married women (in years)		*Sterilized+*		*Practising birth control*		*Not practicing with control*		*Total*	
		GB++	*GR***	*GB*	*GR*	*GB*	*GR*	*GB*	*GR*
25	No. @			6	4	12	10	18	14
	%			33.33	28.6	66.7	71.4	100.0	100.0
25-34	No.	8	10	21	11	23	11	52	32
	%	15.4	31.2	40.4	23.4	44.2	34.4	100.0	100.0
35-44	No.	16	9	7	2	14	10	37	21
	%	43.2	42.9	18.9	9.5	37.3	47.6	100.0	100.0
45+	No.	6	3			5	1	11	4
	%	54.5	75.0			45.5	25.0	100.0	100.0
All ages	No.	30	22	34	17	54	32	118	71
	%	25.4	31.0	28.0	23.9	45.8	45.1	100.0	100.0

* Excluding 26 women in Garhwali Brahman and 14 in Garhwali Rajput who reached menopause and were not interviewed for family planning practices.
\+ Either or both spouses.
++ Garhwali Brahman
** Garhwal Rajput
@ No. of couples.

REFERENCES

Dubey, R.L. and R.P. Srivastava (1965), Trends of Menarche in 367 Women of Uttar Pradesh, *Antrhopologist*, 10:12.

Gosh, P.K. and S. Kumar (1973), Effect of Manarcheal Age on Fertility, *Ind. Anthrop. Soc.*, 8:165.

Gupta, R. (1980), The Sherpa of Upper Khumbu and their migrant counter part in Kalimpong. In : *Man and his Environment*, I.P. Singh and S.C. Tiwari (eds.), New Delhi, Concept Publishing Company.

6

GROWTH AND NUTRITION OF GARHWALI FEMALE CHILDREN

Rekha R. Ghosh

Evaluation of growth and nutritional status of children is generally ascertained by anthropometric measurements, such as stature, and weight. But, circumference of upper arm along with the measurements of skinfold thickness at triceps also serves as a good indicator of growth and nutritional status of a child. Tanner (1962) pointed out that nutrition plays an important decisive role in determining the rate of growth. This idea is also supported by many Indian researchers (Singh, 1964; Madhavan et al., 1967; Rao et al, 1969 and others). Malnutrition also affects the growth rate in children observed by many investigators (Gopalan, 1957; Patwardhan 1961; Rao et al. 1969 and others). Recently, anthropologists have started emphasizing more on the study of growth pattern in relation to food habit and nutrition.

In view of the above idea, an attempt has been made to find out the growth pattern of stature, weight, upper arm circumference and skinfold thickness at triceps among the two important ethnic groups of Garhwal–Brahman and Rajput. The purpose of the study is to find out, in terms of nutrition, growth of the children belonging to a particular age group and also to see whether these two populations differ or agree with each other in the growth trend, magnitude and nutrition.

The cross-sectional data were collected from 240 (120 from each population) school going preadolescent female children between 6 and 10 years of age belonging to Garhwali Brahman and Garhwali Rajput inhabiting Dehradun city and its suburbs. All students belong to almost same socio-economic standards.

The measurements were taken by the author, according to the techniques of Martin (1928) except skinfold thickness which is after Weiner and Laurie, (1969). Skinfold measurement at triceps was measured with the help of UNA Skinfold caliper having a pressure of 10 gm/mm on the contact surface area. The data were divided into four age groups 6-7, 7-8, 8-9 and 9-10 years.

It is evident from Table 1 that stature, weight and upper arm circumference progressively increase from 6-7 years age group to 9-10 years age group in both the populations. Both the populations show the increments in respect of stature and weight through age groups which are statistically significant. Mesurements of skinfold thickness at triceps show a continuous decrease with advancing of age from 6-7 year age group to 9-10 year age group in Brahman while Rajput shows the same trend from 7-8 years to 9-10 years age group instead of the initial age group.

Though the growth trend shows an agreement between Garhwali Brahman and Rajput, yet both the populations differ in magnitudes in corresponding age groups. During the growth period, Brahmans girls are always taller than Rajput in corresponding age groups and also heavier in the first two age groups (6-7 and 7-8 years), thereafter Rajput girls surpass the Brahmans in weight.

In order to evaluate the nutritional status and body measurements, it is clear that both upper arm circumference and skinfold thickness at triceps are greater and thicker respectively in Brahman at the initial age group. Thereafter, there is no consistent pattern between upper arm circumference and skinfold thickness at triceps at the corresponding age groups. It is interesting to note that Rajput girls have greater upper arm circumferences while the fatfold is much thicker in Brahman girls.

Table 1
Statistical Constants: Some Body Measurements

Age Groups (Years)		*Stature (mm)*			*Weight (Kg)*			*Upper arm circumference (mm)*			*Skinfold thickness at triceps (cm)*		
	N	*Mean*	*SD**	*AI**	*Mean*	*SD*	*AI*	*Mean*	*SD*	*AI*	*Mean*	*SD*	*AI*
					GARHWAL RAJPUT								
6-7	30	107.21	2.49		15.43	1.48		14.28	0.91		7.13	1.29	
7-8	30	114.92	2.44	7.71	18.07	2.55	2.64	15.10	1.24	0.82	7.18	1.39	0.05
8-9	30	120.05	2.08	5.13	19.92	2.54	1.85	15.18	1.15	0.08	7.03	1.49	-0.15
9-10	30	126.31	3.10	6.26	23.35	3.78	3.43	16.16	1.25	0.98	6.83	1.72	-0.20
					GARHWALI BRAHMAN								
6-7	30	108.22	3.26		15.50	2.22		14.39	0.83		7.27	1.43	
7-8	30	115.14	2.81	6.92	18.68	3.24	3.18	14.96	1.14	0.57	7.23	1.90	-0.04
8-9	30	120.09	3.27	4.95	19.00	2.66	0.32	15.03	0.97	0.07	7.13	1.71	-0.10
9-10	30	126.90	2.86	6.81	22.50	3.88	3.50	15.87	1.32	0.84	6.73	1.74	-0.41

S.D* = Standard Deviation, A.I.* = Annual Increment

In food habits, Rajput girls are more nonvegetarian (92.6%) than Brahmans (70.8%), while Brahmans are more vegetarian (29.1%) than Rajputs (7.5%). It is clear that the periodicity of different eatables taken by the girls of two populations are not uniformly distributed. Brahaman girls take milk and milk products regularly and occasionally more than Rajput girls but lesser than intake of meat, fish and egg.

It can be concluded from the foregoing results that though Garhwal Brahmans and Garhwali Rajputs living in the same ecozones, migrated from Garhwal Hills more than three generations ago having an almost equal economic status, yet dietary habits and patterns are somewhat different. Greater arm circumferences in Rajput girls may be due to intake of more non vegetarian food than the Brahmans. Similarly, intake of more fatty food, like milk and milk products, in the diet of Brahman children may be the reason for more subcutaneous fat than the Rajput children.

REFERENCES

Gopalan, C. (1957), Malnutrition among infants and young children in India. *J. Trop. Pediat*, 3 :3.

Madhavan, S., T.P. Sushella and M.C. Swaminathan (1967), Association of growth status and the prevalence of nutritional deficiency Signs among pre-school children. *Ind. J. Med. Res.*, 5: 499.

Martin, R. (1928), *Lehrbuch der Anthropologie*, Gustav Fischer, Njena.

Patwardhan, N.V. (1961), Nutrition in India, *Ind. J. Med. Res.* Publication, 2nd Edition, 228.

Rao, N.P., D. Singh and M.C. Swaminathan (1969), Nutritional Status of Pre-school Children of Rural Communities Near Hyderabad City, *Ind. J. Med. Res.* 57: 432.

Singh, R. (1964), Nutritional Somatometric Study of Adult Males with Special Reference to Skinfold Measurements and Correlation. In *Aspect of Indian Anthropolgy*, (ed.) P.C.

Biswas and I.P. Singh, Dept. of Anthropology, Delhi University, Delhi, 173.

Tanner, J.M. (1962), *Growth at Adolescence*. Oxford, Blackwell Scientific Publications.

Weiner, J.S. & J.A. Laurie 1969. *Human Biology: A Guide to Field Methods*, IBP, Hand Book No. 9, Oxford, Blackwell Scientific Publications.

7

DELINATIONS FROM THE ETHNO-RELIGIOUS MOSSAIC OF DEHRADUN

G. S. Bhatt

In the Indian situation, the term ethnic would include groups defined and delineated by *jati* (caste), region-language (*desh*), *mat-panth*, and even nationality (the Tibbetan and the Parsi for example). Quite often these groupings mutually cut across and criss-cross in Dehradun, for example, *Shaiva Mat* cuts across the Garhwali and the non-Garhwali. Islam cuts across the Gujar. The Banjara, though Muslim by faith, are commonly referred to as the Banjara which, broadly speaking, identifies them as a *Jati*.

From this perspective, Dehradun may be said to have had its ethnic origin. By derivation, Dehradun would mean the Dun (the valley) in which the Dehra (the tomb/the cenotaph) of Shri Guru Ram Rai is located. Ram Rai was the eldest son of the Sikh *Guru* (Har Rai) of the Sikh. Ram Rai's closeness with Aurangzeb could not help him in his battle of succession to the *Guru-Gaddi*. After the execution of Guru Tegh Bahadur, for political reasons, Aurangzeb instructed Ram Rai to leave Delhi and retire to the wilderness of the Dun' (Walton, 1911).

In the Dun, under the patronage of Aurangzeb and Garhwal rulers, Ram Rai hoisted the flag of his spiritual-religious authority and found the *gurudwara* of *Udasi Panth*.

After him, this *gurudwara* grew into Darbar Shri Guru Ram Rai. In the rear part of it are located the Dehras of Guru Ram Rai and his four wives. It became the nucleus of the Dehra of yester years and the Dehradun of today. In the early records of the British, Dehradun is more frequently referred to as Dehra (Walton, 1911).

Methodologically, Dehra's origin may be attributed to a socio-political stride of history, precipitated in the plains from Delhi to Punjab and by the growing distance and conflict between Aurangzeb and the Sikhs. Historically, many other strides, growing in and around the Dun, have left their respective indelible marks on the religio-ethnic composition of the Dun and Dehra. Founding of Ashokan Rock Edict at Kalsi, Invasions of Tymore, Shahjahan (the Mughal), the Ruhela and the Maratha, emergence and consolidation of Garhwal Princedom, colonization and founding of feudatories by the Banjara, the Gujar and the Pundir, occupation by the Gurkha (1803-1814), and the British (1814-1947), India's independence and partition are some crucial strides of history.

Geo-political location of the Dun made these strides and their consequences possible. Both geographically and historically, the Dun has not been a closed valley. Its passes at Haridwar, Kansro, Mohand and Timli connect it to Indo-Gangetic plains. Through these passes came invaders, marauders, travelers, refugees, colonizers and harbingers of *mat-panth*. The Dun does not break but extends the transportation lines from the plains to the Hills. It has been a socio-political buffer, a zone of acculturation between diverse ethnic elements and of transit of ethnic influences from the plains and the hills.

Besides, Dehradun's religio-ethnic composition has grown in the backdrop of the organic relationship between the Dun and the Dehra. In its growth, Dehra, primarily, drew from the resources of the Dun. Jakhan and Rajpur, once prosperous trading centers, lost their trade and were subsequently engulfed by Dehra. Bangal, near Sahastradhara, dwindled as a trading centre. Members of Nangal's trading community migrated to Dehra and became the Nagalia Baniya of

Dehradun. The Mirotha of Nangal are said to be the descendants of the Maratha settlers who took local wives.

With improvement in the means of transportation and communication under the British and after independence, Dehra made a tremendous growth. From a grown up village of 518 houses and 2,106 individuals, when the British occupied it, Dehra has grown into an ethnically heterogenous metropolis of five lac or more individuals, spatially divided into thrityfour wards, with each ward having ethnically identifiable mohallas/localities. Initially drawing from the local resources of the Dun, Dehra, subsequently, drew on the ethnic and demographic resources of the plains, surrounding the Dun. After independence, its tentacles became longer but thinner.

THE SETTING OF DESH AND JATI

The grouping based on language - region (*desh* in the colloquial usage) and its caste-identities, seem to be basic to Dehra's ethnic setting. In this setting *mat-panth* and cult align and/or cut across or criss-cross the *desh-jati* groupings. Using the concept of *desh*, some ten broad ethnic groupings can be identified in Dehradun's population.

The immigrants from the mountainous terrain, spreading to the north-west of the Dun, can be identified as the Garhwali, the Himachali-Jaunsari (including those from Rawain-Jaunpur), the Gorkhali and the Tibbeti. Those from the plains of Sindhu and Ganga are identified as the Punjabi, the Khuravi (along with the Hariyanvi and the Ruhelvi, and Awadhi-Bhojpuri, the Purbia) respectively. Immigrants from far-flung linguistic regions like the Bengali-Oriya, the Gujarati-Marathi and the speakers of Dravidian languages and the Parsi constitute small communities.

Among the small communities, the Bengali are the earliest immigrants. Among them, the Brahmin and the Kayastha–the two upper castes of Bengali–are most numerous. They came as government servants and established the Bengali mohalla. With the Bengali came the powerful impact of the *shakti-cult*.

The speakers of Dravidian languages are a microscopic minority. By and large, they remain as mobile migrants to the city. They come as professionals and government servants in the scientific institutions of the central government. They form a part of the city's middle classes drawn from diverse linguistic-regional communities. Same is the case with the Gujarati and the Marathi. However, a lowly placed Gujarati speaking community, gradually, has carved out a place in the city's economic life. The women of this community sell utensils by exchanging them with old, discarded clothes. The men mend these clothes and sell them in the market which has grown adjacent to the Pavilion Ground, near Gandhi Park.

The Himachal do not seem to have exerted as much ethnic influence on the Dun as they did on neighbouring Jaunsar Bawar and Rawain. It is reported that, in recent time, many Himachalis and Jaunsaris have purchased land near Vikasnagar (formerly Chuharah Pur) and settled as cultivators. However, with the growth in education and benefits of reservation in govt. services, the incidence of Jaunsaris settling in the city has been on the increase. Its extent, however, has not been worked out.

The Gorkhali are settled in Garhi-Dakra and Jakhan and in the villages (Narwal and Raipur for example) around the city. Mostly, they are descendants of the Gurkha recruited in the British Army, who settled in the Dun after retirement. They are stratified into the Brahmin (Upadhyaya, Sharma, Joshi etc.) and the Kshatri (Gurung, Magar, Kshetri, Thapa, Rana, Mal etc.) castes with the latter having numerical and social predominance over the former.

The Tibbeti are not Indian nationals but refugees. Over the last three decades, their settlements have grown up on the periphery of Dehradun's municipality from Rajpur to Gujarrha and Clement Town. The Tibbeti market along the boundary of erstwhile Rangers College is indicative of their integration with the city's economy. They have contributed their technique and motifs of making woolen carpets. They have also brought with them the *Boudha Mat* as it acculturated in Tibbet.

The Garhwali are most predominant in city's population. The highest incidence of their migration is from Paurhi district–the erstwhile British Garhwal followed by the districts of Tehri and Chamoli. A good number of them are migrants from the surrounding villages. Among the Garhwali, the *savarna*–the Brahmin and the Rajput–dominate both numerically and socially. Immigration of the Garhwali Harijan (Artisan, and labour castes, is scant. Since, in the city, they hide their castes, a proper assessment of their immigration to the city is difficult.

Among the Garhwali, though casually, a distinction is also more between the Kathmali and the Garhwali–rather, the pure Garhwali as the commonly used phrase goes. The pure Garhwali are those who speak undiluted Garhwali and maintain link with the place of migration. The Kathmali being very early migrants, generally, do not speak Garhwali. They have adopted many a customs not followed in the hills–one example being the observation of the festive ritual of *karwa chauth* by Garhwali women, settled in the city since long.

The Punjabi are, more or less, equally dominant ethnic element. The Sikh swept through the valley in 1775 and 1783 but they never attempted to settle here (Walton, 1911). With the partition of the country, Dehradun saw a heavy influx of the Sikh and the non-Sikh Punjabi. Among the latter the Bannoowals (the migrants from Bannoo Kohat who spoke Pashto, are said to be numerous. The Panjabi, as whole, are dominated by the Jat and the Khatri who, along with many lower orders, cut across the Sikh and non-Sikh (now commonly referred to as the Sikh and the Hindu).

A small Yadav community, dairy keepers, too migrated to Dehradun as Panjabi-Pasthto speaking group from Bahnoo-Kohat. In their households, they speak Awadhi. Settled in Dehradun, Saharanpur, Ambala and other cities of Panjab, their women retain old Awadhi dress. In observing rites of passage, they are set in the matrix of Awadhi *deshachar*. They recall being migrants from Awadh (round about Sitapur) at the time of mutiny.

The Khuravi, along with Ruheli and Hariyanvi, region is contiguous to the Dun. It surrounds it from east to south-west as the geographical necklace to the Dun and Siwaliks. Most notable among the migrants from these regions are the Gujar, the Rajput (the Pundir), the Baniya (the Aggarwal, the Rajvanshi and the Jain). The Gujar and the Rajput reclaimed land and established villages in Dun in the first quarter of eighteenth century. They also entered the Dun as *marauders* when Garhwal Rulers were weak (Walton, 1911).

The Jat, the Pal (the shephered caste) and the Tyagi also hail from this region. Among the low castes, the Chamar are numerically noteworthy. Identifying as the Raidasi, they are drawn from a vast rural hinterland covering the districts of Saharanpur, Roorkee and Bijnor, with the Bijnori being most numerous among them. They are partly mobile and partly settled and occupationally heterogenous.

The Jatiya, a small Chamar community, are confined to Jatiya Mohalla on the periphery of old Dehra. They are reported to be migrants from erstwhile Gawalior State, somewhere in the middle of nineteenth century. Retaining their traditional occupation of working in leather, they are a settled group in the city.

Walton traces the influx of Muslims in the Dun mainly from Delhi, Saharanpur and Bijnore with minor contributions from other neighbouring plain districts. According to him, the four upper castes–Sheikh, Saiyyad, Mughal and Pathan–are numerically important. The Pathan came with the invasion of Ruhela Najibulla. In numerical strength, the Banjara, the Teli and the Mirasi come after the upper castes. Nominalistic castes like Ghosi, Jullahas, Nais, Mullas, Kassabs, Bhishtis, Lohars, Manihars, Fakirs, Behnas and Kanjars are present but not important numerically.

This portrayal of the Muslim by Walton may not be available today. The Muslim Nai from Gonda district, speaking Awadhi, would be classed as the Purbia. In recent years, Muslim migrants from Bihar have been added to the city's ethnic composition with their small localities which have sprung up on banks of Rispana. The Muslim are highly concentrated in and around the Inamulla Building. They are an economically heterogeneous community.

The Purbia are said to have migrated to Dehradun first as recruits in the British Army and then as labour in tea-plantation and construction of railway line. The contemporary influx of labour from Balia and Bihar indicates that Dehradun's pull for the Purbia has not subsided. As they say, they are lured by higher wages.

Though partly settled and partly mobile and migratory, on the whole, the Purbia maintain a closer link with the place (*desh*) of their migration. Yet, they reclaimed land and established villages in the Dun (Harrawala) for example. Many Purbia settlements on the banks of Rispana and Bindal rivers–like Chirhiya Mandi, Barighat and Nayagaon–are Dehradun's Mohallas.

Among the Purbia the castes of the middle and lower levels predominate. The Lodh, the Yadava, the Kurmi, the Kumhar, the Barhai, the Rajbhar and the Barai are the castes of the middle level–the backward as the current politicized definition goes. The Khatik, the Jaiswar, the Kori, the and Chamar (Kanaujiya in Bihar) fall in the lower level. The Purbia's contribution to the city's middle and professional classes–comparatively speaking–is scarce. They mostly work in unskilled and semi-skilled occupations.

MAT-PANTH AND CULTS

The fossil remains of Ramapithecus and Siwapithecus and excavation of Paleolithic tools near Kalsi, testify to the pre-historic antiquity of the Dun. However, because of the scarcity of extensive and sound archaeological evidence, not much is known about the religio-ethnic traits of the pre-historic inhabitants of the Dun. On the other hand, Dun's popular history, based on oral traditions, needs a critical examination in the methodological perspective of comparative ethnography based on Indology. As for example, does Dun derive its name from its association with Dronacharya of Mahabharat? Again, is Lakshman Siddha, along with other Siddhas, indicative of the impact of Siddha tradition or Dun's association with Lakshman, the younger brother of Ram?

Extent and depth of *Baudha Mat* in the valley is uncertain and elusive. It is yet not finally decided if Ashokan rock edict at Kalsi marks the boundary between Scythean Nagas of the hills and kings of the plains; or is it an indicator of widespread popular observance of *Baudha Mat*? Or, is it simply a medium of diffusing and popularizing the ethnical exhortations of Ashok? The *Budha Mat* of Tibbetan refugees is confined to them only. There is a need to dive deeper in the ethnographic material of the valley to delineate the traces of *Budha Mat*.

The *Jain mat* does not seem to be as ancient to the valley. Available information indicates that it might have diffused into the valley along with its followers who, overwhelminghly, belong to the Bania castes. They mostly follow the *Digambar Marg*. Though economically diversified and having a wider network of inter-community interaction, they are a well-knit 'sama' bound by Jain-ideology, festivals and cults. *Jain mandirs* are located in Jain Dharmshala, Sarnimal house, Bhanda Mohalla, Rajpur and Clement Town. Among these, those of Sarnimal house and Jhanda Mohalla are said to be the oldest. They stand on the periphery of Dehra's nucleus where the Jains concentrate.

Presence of *Vedic yagya* tradition is borne out by the excavation of a *yagnashala*, near Kalsi. Shakti, Shiva, Ram and Krishna cults have been reinforced in the valley through successive migrations from the plains of such groups as observed them. These cults cut across caste, regional and even panthic groupings. Janmashtami, for example, is an important festival of the followers of Shivanaraini panth. Social celebration of Basant Panchami is popular with the Bangali and the Shivanaraini. For the former, it is an occasion of Saraswati Puja while for the latter, it is that of *gurupuja*.

Celebration of Durgashtami in the month of Ashwin (Oct-Nov.) and Chaitra (April) is household festive ritual with

Hindus drawn from diverse linguistic regions and even panthic affiliations. On these occasions, the fair of Shakumbri Devi in the district of Saharanpur attracts almost all the communities of all the linguistic regions as a matter of devotion-cum-excursion and economic interest in the case of pedlars. The pompous *jagra* (worship of Shakti) of the Punjabi is making in roads in other communities.

Communal celebration of Durgashtami in the month of Ashwin is very popular and strong with the Bangali and the Gorkhali. The Gurkha unit in cantonment retains the tradition of buffalo-sacrifice. The *Durga Puja* of the Bangali attracts devotees from other communities as well.

Sanjhi may be described as a *desachari* (regional) tradition of Shakti-cult. In the celebration of *Sanjhi*, clay-idols of the goddess (*Sanjhi*) and other motifs are modelled, dried, coloured and fixed on the wall as a pattern of tiles-*murmal*. Worship of *Sanjhi* goes on through out *navaratra*. It is essentially a woman's art and ritual.

In the city, *Sanjhi* is celebrated by the migrants from Roorkee, Saharanpur, Muzaffar Nagar and Meerut districts and among such castes as the Baniya, the Gujar, the Darji, the Pall and the Tyagi. Though a household ritual, it is not celebrated in each and every house, a male in Dela Ram Bazar, has cultivated the art of modeling *Kharhi Sanjhi* (Standing *Sanjhi*) on the Bangali style of modeling *Durga*.

The Shiva-cult is equally pervasive though it is an outstanding Gorkhali trait. The highly popular and most frequented temple, Tapkeshwar, now included in the itinerary of city's tourists, stands near Garhi-Dakra where the Gorkhali concentrate. Yet, *Shivaratri* fair at Tapkeshwar is not essentially a Gorkhali fair. It draws from other communities as well. It is a big draw for the Purbia who participate in it with their colourful and characteristic style of singing *bhag*.

Celebration of *Ram Lila* may be taken as an expression of Rama-cult. Four Rama Lilas are staged in the city. The one staged in Shivaji Dharamshala is said to be the oldest. It was formerly staged in Rama Lila Bazar which is a part of Dehra's nucleus. It is managed by the Baniya. The one staged in

Kallumal Dharamshala is an offshoot of it. The Ram Lila staged in Chukhuwala is known as the Ram Lila of the Garhwali and the one staged in the municipal grounds is managed by the Bannoowals. Observation of the ritual fast to be celebrated *Ramanawami* (birth anniversary of Bhagwan Ram) seems to be more popular with the Purbia, particularly those drawn from the region of Awadh. It is an important festival of the *Kabirpanthis* whose presence is feeble in the city.

Krishna-cult finds expression in the celebration of *Janmashtami* (birth anniversary of Bhagwan Krishna). It is celebrated at family and community levels. In the city, at the family level, *Janmashtami sajana* (depicting glimpses from Krishna's life) with the help of toys, a stone, colours and vegetation available, is children's affair in which elders help. In this annual festive arrangement of *Janmashtami* of more interest is innovation of traditional motifs and introduction of new ones, particularly those from contemporary life and immediate habitat.

At D.L. Road has come up Shri Chaitanya Gaudiya Math. It is devoted to Krishna-cult. It is one of the chain of such *maths* established in important cities of India and abroad. It is run under a Trust with restricted membership. Its clergy is drawn from higher castes though it is open to all. The public feast arranged on the third day of Krishna *Janmashtami* is open to all irrespective of caste and creed.

PANTHIC TRADITIONS

Darbar Shri Guru Ram Rai represents the tradition of *Udasi Panth*. Paying obeisance at the tomb of its founder and to the presiding *mahant* and observation of the Jhanda cult are its main features. Being a zamindari as well, the Darbar remained pivotal to Dehera's civic life till independence. Geographically, its following ranges from cis-Sutlaj region to Moradabad, Laksar, Roorkee, Saharanpur and now even abroad. As in all other *nirgunis bhakti panths*, its followers, too, are drawn mostly from lower castes. The annual congregational fair of the Darbar, the Jhanda Mela, draws from all the communities of the city. Under the present *mahant*, the Darbar has made notable contributions towards the cause of education for all.

The panthic tradition of Guru Govind Singh was overwhelmingly introduced in the city after partition. The socio-religious life of the followers of this tradition revolves round the *gurudwaras* that have come up in the localities where the Sikh have tended to concentrate. The social service performed by the gurudwara in the form of lending of utensils and beddings to its members as well as to those on nominal charges has grown into a social matrix of intra-community interaction and understanding.

The Bijnori Chamar of the city offer an interesting example of interpenetration and criss-crossing of various *mat-panths* within the confinement of the same caste. They identified themselves as Raidesi indicating their allegiance to Raidas panth. The impact of Simla mat differentiated them into two panthic streams–*Bai Ke Sikh* (Nanak Panthi) and *Guru Ke Sikh* (the followers of Guru Govind Singh). Then they imbibed the impact of *Arya Samaj*. Now many of them are drawn towards *Baudha mat* as enunciated by Ambedkar. One can also notice a feeble throwback of Sikh panth among them. They celebrate the birth anniversary of Ravidas and Ambedkar. Observing Shiva, Krishna and Karwa-cults, they provide a good following to the Jhanda-Darbar-cult of Shri Guru Ram Rai.

The Purbia have diffused into the city as *Shivanaraini* and *Kabir panths* with *Shivanarainis* being more numerous. The *Shivanarainis* are mainly drawn from Jaiswar and Kori castes, the members of which intermarry also. Among the local *Shivanarainis,* the number of the Dusadh and Dhobi is feeble. Organizationally, Mohalla *gurudwaras* are linked to the central Shivanaraini *gurudwara,* standing on E.C. Road in the vicinity of DAV College.

The followers of *Radhaswami mat* are drawn mostly from the Punjabi and Khuravi communities but with a pronounced tilt towards the former. The local Radhaswamis are differentiated on the basis of allegiance to two *gaddis*–Agra and Taran Taran. Among them the Khatri are reported to outnumber the others.

Manav Kendra at Saharanpur Road, *Bramh Kumari* Kendra at Rajpur Road, the *Path of Mehr Baba* and a number of Ashrams located beyond Rajpur (like *Shahanshahi Ashram*) appear to be offshoots of the *Nirgunia Bhakti Marg* which dominated the Indian worldwide in the later medieval period.

Ram Tirth Ashram, Ram Krishna Mission and *Arya Samaj* represent the waves of religio-social reform movements generated in the nineteenth century. Ram Krishna Mat is a recent addition. It diffused with recent Bangali migrants. Arya Samaj was founded in the city after the first visit of Dayanad Saraswati. The Arya Samaj Mandir of Tapovan was established by a Sikh which is now run under a trust. Non-trust refugees from Panjab reinforced Arya Samaj in the city.

The Kayasth and the Baniya were early harbingers of Arya Samaj in Dehradun. The Jat joined them later. The Khatri were more numerous among the non-Sikh refugees from Panjab, followed by the Brahmin and the Baniya. The Arya Samaj made its impact through its programme of conversion, reconversion and reclaimation and also through its movement of religio-social reforms mainly aimed at promotion of education, woman's uplift and redemption of untouchables and protest against idol-worship.

The pronounced influence of Islam in the city's social composition dwindled after partition. The *majar* cult, more popular with non-Muslims, seems to have derived from the *Sufi-marg. Majar,* too, means tomb/shrine. More worshipped are five Saiyad *majars.* Those are located in the compound of old Rangers' College, Survey of India compound of Hathi Barkhala, Chorkhala, Lakkhi Bag and adjacent to civil hospital, facing the municipality.

Each of these *majars* is known after the saint enshrined in it. The one near the hospital is known after one Kmaluddin Shah. Its homage is most popular. A *majar* on Old Survey Road is also said to be that of a Saiyad but it is small and anonymous and not so popular. Here and there, anonymous *majars* are found in some houses. The owner of such a house, might light a lamp at night and place it at the *majar* of his house. The *majar-*

cult comes nearer to Dehra-cult. If the ritual worship of the Siddha-cult at *Lakshama Siddha* is taken into account, a comparison of three cults is academically inviting.

By the time Walton (1911) wrote his account of Dehra, there had been a substantial increase in the Christian population of the valley. The city's Christian population consisted of native converts and of Europeans or European extraction. Methodists, Anglicans, Presbyterians and Roman Catholics were then successful missionary communities. Dehra-Mission, a branch of American Mission of Ludhiana, grew into Indian Church of Dehra. Reformed Presbyterian Church at Dehra became an indigenous institution. How these churches have been interacting in the process of unity in diversity is a matter of investigation which this author could not undertake.

Christian Mission(s) made a notable contribution towards the education. The pattern of management of the English medium public schools seems to have been borrowed largely from the convent schools. The Christian Retreat and Study Centre at Rajpur (Masihi/Dhyan Kendra), near Shahanshahi Ashram, is devoted to the study of comparative religion and the doctrine and technique of evangelism with a focus on Christian mission(s).

NOTES

1. Where a system of thought, relating to the supernatural and/or its negation is propounded after the experience of a historical person–sometimes considered divine–or after the concept of a God and a system of his worship (Shiva, Vishnu and Shakti for example), or after a well-propounded philosophy, it grows into a mat (viewpoint). The latter may socially crystallize into *sangh/samaj/panth*. There cannot be a *panth* without its corresponding mat. Meaning the way, the concept of *mat-panth* may be extended to cover even Christianity and Islam and can be used as a synonym of religion.
2. Guru Ram Rai hoisted the flag and founded the *gurudwara* at Dhammawala. It formed a part of the *jagir*, granted to him by the then ruler of Garhwal. It was situated near Khurburha and both of them are older than Dehra. However, today Darbar is bound

by Bhandari Chowk, Darshani Gate, Sharanpur Chowk and Jhanda Mohalla.

3. The Rajput of Jaunsar Bawar and also of Rawain claim to be immigrants from the erstwhile princedoms of Jubbal, Taronch and Rampur Bushahar etc. Very little reference is made of Nahen though politically, it controlled Jaunsar Bawar in medieval period. In contrast to this, the Brahmin of Jaunsar Bawar traces their migration to Rawain and those of Rawain to Tehri state.
4. In a survey done by the author, a few families of Pant Brahmins from Kumaun identified themselves as Garhwali. Being settled in Garhwal since long, they were fluent in Garhwali.
5. The Shiva temple, near Ghantaghar, is said to have been constructed by the Gurkha in the British Army. That of Paltan Bazar is organizationally linked to the temple of Tapkeshwar. There is an old Shiva temple at Jakhan. Many new Shiva Temples have come up in new localities. Not much is known about ethnic affiliation and social organization of these temples.

REFERENCES

Walton, H.G. (1911), Dehradun: A Gazetteer, Vol. I, Allahabad, Govt., Press.

Souvenier (1980), Arya Samaj Dehradun Centenary.

8

COMMUNAL HARMONY IN DEHRADUN CITY

Zainab Rehman

Communal harmony and peaceful co-existence are two essential ingredients of a prosperous pluralistic society and their significance in contemporary Indian society can hardly be overemphasized. Internal peace and order is necessary for any nation or society to make progress and derive maximum benefits from its assets; secondly, achievements and progress can be maximum when all members of the society cooperate and make united efforts. In recent times our country has suffered great losses, in more than one sense due to communal discord; so much so that all right minded Indians are making all our efforts to achieve communal harmony.

Dehradun, a peaceful and cosmopolitan place, presents a good example of communal harmony and mutual cooperation. It is inhabited by people of different religions. My research was related to the Muslims of Dehradun, who constitute about 8 per cent of the city's population. These Muslims are scattered all over the city and belong to different socio-economic status. Muslims have been living in Dehradun for centuries. Probably the Muslim population was most prosperous in the 18th century, when Dehradun was under Muslim rule. After the death of Najib-du-Daula, who had occupied Dehradun in 1757, the city was attacked by many invaders and finally came under the rule of the Gurkhas of Nepal. The British, who started a war with Nepal, got Dehradun when the war ended with the signing of the treaty of Bagauli. At the time of partition of the country, Dehradun also witnessed rioting and bloodshed. An old resident, who was an active member of the Congress at the time of independence said that about half the population of Dehradun was Muslim before partition. Due to prevailing conditions, many prosperous Muslims migrated to Pakistan, while many refugees came from across the border and settled in Dehradun, including both Sikhs and Hindus. Thus the percentage of Muslims in Dehradun population decreased considerably. Still, there are quite a few well to do Muslims in Dehradun who have been living here for past many generations; but their number is very small as compared to the number of Muslims who belong to the low socio economic group. This group includes artisans, masons, fruit and vegetable vendors, and petty shopkeepers. Among the middle class local Muslims, some members are educated and engaged in a good job here or abroad. Besides, the Muslims who originally belong to Dehradun, there is another Muslim group which is quite significant because they are economically well off and are in Govt. service and liked the place so much that they decided to settle here. There is sizeable number of middle class and upper middle class who have made Dehradun their home town and have been living here for the past two or three decades. Most of them have constructed their houses too. Thus in this cosmopolitan city we find Muslims from different parts of the country, though mostly from UP, settling down as its inhabitants. This is one reason why Muslim culture in Dehradun is composite and varied.

One of the objectives of my research was to find out what status was given to Muslims by people of their own community as well as people of other communities. The information collected in this regard throws some light on communal harmony, as it exists in Dehradun. A majority of respondents, 67 per cent to be precise, felt that Muslims in India are not given equal status in all spheres of life, but only 31.50 per cent said they had faced some form of discrimination themselves, while 66.50 per cent said they hadn't. This shows that respondents feel that Muslims are much less discriminated against in Dehradun than in other parts of the country. This was further proved by the fact that 84 per cent respondents said that they feel their non Muslim neighbours consider their families as sociable. 86.50 per cent respondents said they have close and intimate relations with their immediate neighbours, about half of them being non-Muslim, as 51 per cent respondents have either both or atleast non-Muslim immediate neighbour.

Questions pertaining to friends also highlighted good relations with non-Muslims. 69.50 per cent respondents said they have friends belonging to all religions and 3.50 per cent said they have mostly non-Muslim friends. Only 13.00 per cent said they have mostly Muslim friends. This shows that most of the Muslims in Dehradun have non Muslim friends. 76.50 per cent respondents said that they visit or meet their friends frequently and always dine together without any hesitation. This shows that a majority of Muslims mix freely with non-Muslim friends. In response to the query regarding whose help is sought first in emergency or difficult times, 50.0 per cent said from immediate neighbours, while another 23.50 per cent said from neighbours as well as other friends and relatives. Once again we see a majority of Muslims seeking help from neighbours and friends in times of difficulty regardless of their religion.

Besides all these data there are some interesting case studies those show how people of all religions get along very well in Dehradun. One female respondent, who was poor and uneducated told that poor people, belonging to any religion, always realise each others problems and go out of their way to help one another, if not monetarily, then by giving moral support; while the rich cannot identify with the problems and circumstances of the poor, irrespective of their religion. In her difficult times, the Pradhan of their locality who is a non-Muslim, has helped her; besides all her neighbours, both Hindus and Muslims, have always stood by her. She is a domestic servant and works for people of all religions. Here too, some of her non-Muslim employers are very kind to her.

Sometimes they have gone out of their way to help her. She has been tying a *Raakhi* every year to a non-Muslim gentleman, whom she really considers a brother and who has taken care of her children and helped her in many ways in the past. Another female respondent, who is slightly educated and works in a vocational centre, said for herself Hindus and Muslims are alike and she feels there should be no such distinction. A Hindu social worker has done so much for her that she is more grateful to her than to anyone else. The views of an aged respondent, who was an influential Congress member during the period of Independence and partition, are worth noting. He said, before Independence, when Hindus and Muslims were in nearly equal numbers, there was great communal harmony. At the time of partition the communal feeling flared up and it took a couple of years for normalcy to be restored. But, he feels the old feeling of brotherhood is not as strong as it was earlier. Even then, he concedes that conditions are better here than in other cities of UP. Also many personal friendships between people of different religions have withstood the ravages of time and adverse conditions. He also feels that now, Muslims are a very small number in Dehradun city, and have little power or influence personally. Therefore probably the community is not considered as a force to reckon with.

Informal talks with respondents and their family members showed that many of them feel that communal feelings and feeling of insecurity and mistrust were generated to a great extent in the last few years when the Babri Masjid issue gained national significance. Data were collected in the latter half of 1990, and communal harmony was in grave danger towards the fag end of that year. But it is heartening to note that even at that time many respondents were quite optimistic and satisfied with their status and condition.

Various factors were found to be responsible for better communal harmony in Dehradun. First of all the very high literacy rate and prevalent intellectual atmosphere in the city has created a liberal and positive outlook among all citizens. Citizens are interested in leading peaceful and prosperous lives.

Education has taught people of all religions to tolerate and adapt, to co-exist and cooperate.

Secondly, most Muslims in Dehradun are exposed to people of different religious and cultural background and learn many new practices as well as ideas from them. Their contacts and friendship with different types of people has made them more tolerant, more liberal and more amenable to change. This factor was noticed not only to affect the educated but also the uneducated and poor Muslims. In fact many poor Muslims, who are also uneducated, have adapted very well to changing circumstances and adopted liberal and tolerant attitudes because it is necessary for their survival. They have also realised the benefits of accepting change and giving up their old customs which prevent them from making progress in the modern world. For instance, many poor women have given up the use of *Burqa* as it is not practical now, most poor and uneducated Muslims are now educating their children, both sons and daughters. Women have started taking up jobs in various capacities and have become more confident and self-sufficient. All these changes have brought the Muslims in the national mainstream and they are interacting with people from all regions and backgrounds in their professional and social life. Due to similar occupations, education, life style and preferences, friendships develop between people of different regions and religions and they learn not only to accept each others' way of life but also adopt some practices they like. These close contacts and friendships contribute to communal harmony.

Another factor that has contributed to a communal harmony by making many Muslims in Dehradun liberal minded and friendly with people of other communities is that many of them, especially those in Govt. service, do not originally belong to Dehradun; they are living away from their relatives. Hence their friends and neighbours, whether Muslims or non-Muslims, mean a lot to them. They seek their company, help and advice, whenever necessary. Thus they become very close to each other. Secondly, absence of relatives and elders in the city, (*Biradari*), enables the young and even not so young, Muslim couples to leave or give up old customs that are not compatible with modern times and adopt new and modern life style and mix freely with every one. Thus the pressure of elders to maintain old customs, or in other words their traditionalizing influence, is lacking. This leads both Muslim men and women to have more freedom to choose friends, change their life style and in general be more modern and broad minded.

Although my research was confined to Muslims, having lived in Dehradun for two decades and being friendly with people of different background I presume that most probably similar factors have also made people of other communities in Dehradun more broad minded and tolerant. As a result, Dehradun, fortunately presents a very peaceful and harmonious environment for all its inhabitants.

9

INDUSTRIAL DEVELOPMENT OF DISTRICT DEHRADUN

B. N. S. Bhatnagar

Industries, rural or urban, large or small, play a potent role not merely in creating employment but also in generating a process of sustained development. Industrial units of organised sector generally provide life blood to the economic system by their leading role in transmitting growth impulses to the surrounding areas through their backward and forward linkages. The underdeveloped regions have observed that there is a strong and positive connection between the wealth and standard of living of a country and the extent of its industrialization (Murray 1960). On the other hand, inadequate development of industrial sector is both an indicator and cause of backwardness. Hence, industrial development has become one of the great crusades of our time.

The district of Dehradun nestles in the lap of the Himalayas with a charming sylvan setting and a distinct geographical entity. It is bounded on the North East by the Himalayas, on the South West by the river Yamuna and on the South East by the river Ganga. Geographically, the sauccershaped Doon Valley lies between $29^{0}57'$ and $31^{0}2'3''$ north latitude and $77^{0}34'45''$ and $78^{0}18'30''$ east longitude.

In 1980s, Doon Valley was recommended to be declared an ecologically fragile zone and thereafter various authorities have imposed a number of restrictions on the esablishment and expansion of new industries. These restrictions have resulted in an arrest of all developmental activities which have been at a stand still since 1989. Therefore, an attempt has been made in this paper to review the industrial development of Dehradun district and to suggest potential areas of industrial development to fulfil the needs of development.

RESOURCES

The soil, natural resources and the climate of the area are the main natural factors in the evolution of all economic activities including industrial development. Hence, it would be appropriate to briefly discuss the resources of the district. The hinterland of Dehradun is richly endowed with natural resources like minerals, forests and fertile agricultural land. The important minerals constitute limestone, gypsum, tufa, copper, lead-gold phosphorrite, marble, slates and quartzites. Apart from minerals, many types of forests with different varieties of trees are found in Dehradun district. The lowest slopes of Shivaliks, where the proportion of clay is larger and the drainage better, provide the best soils for the growth of *sal* trees. *Sal* forest is grown on vast tracts upto an altitude of 1300 metres. *Sal* is the main timber species which is converted into scantlings, railway sleepers, planks and other constructional purposes. Amongst other forests, *chir, deodear, jamun, khair-sisam, semal, tun, bamboo* and eucalyptus are most common and are found in a mixed pattern, except *chir* and *deodar* forests. Dehradun is located at Dehra plateau which occupies the most fertile land of district Dehradun. The whole of this tract is irrigated by canals. The best quality of wheat and rice is grown here and sugarcane, onions, tobacco and strawberries also grow abundantly.

The beauty and climate of Doon Valley have also provided the natural potential for a prosperous tourist industry (Bandyopadhyay and Shiva, 1984). Its location amidst the picturesque Doon Valley at the foothills of outer Himalayan ranges has effected the economic viability of the city in a positive way. The entire Doon Valley is full of places of scenic beauty and picnic spots like Sahastradhara, Robber's cave, Tapkeshwar Mahadev Temple, Malsi Deer Park, Raipur Spring, Raja ji wild life Sanctuary etc. Rivers and springs are yet other important resources which provide irrigation and fishing facilities. Mussoorie provides spots of great natural scenic beauty with its levish forests and flowing springs. In addition, the valley's location as the gateway to the famous pilgrim centers of Kedarnath, Badrinath, Yamunotri-Gangotri also attract a huge number of tourists. This combination of health, pilgrimage and recreation based tourism has made Doon Valley a popular tourist resort which has a significant contribution to the economy of the valley (Bandyopadhyay and Shiva, 1984). Hence, Dehradun is endowed with rich mineral, forest resources, agriculture and climatic conditions. All these factors have helped Dehradun to become a good centre for institutions of excellence.

Dehradun has a number of institutes of national level such as Forest Research Institute (now a Deemed University), Indian Institute of Petroleum, Survey of India, Ordnance Factory, Indian Military Academy, Headquarters of Oil and Natural Gas Corporation, Malviya Institute of Petroleum Exploration, Institute of Drilling Technology, Central Soil and Water Conservation Institute, Wadia Institute of Himalayan Geology, Indian Institute of Remote Sensing, Anthropological Survey of India, Lal Bahadur Shahstri (which provides the human resource for administration) etc.

Besides the professional training institutes, Dehradun also has a comparative advantage for institutions which impart schooling to a large number of students. As a result of the existence of schools and higher research and training institutions, Dehradun has an extremely high rate of literacy (69.5 per cent in 1991) which is among the highest in the entire country. Keeping in view all these factors Dehradun has been placed under the 'High' category of development on the basis of composite index of overall development based on agriculture, industry, academic infra-structure and social services indicators for the reference period 1970-71 and 1980-81 (Tewari, 1984). Thus, Dehradun is one of the highly developed districts of the state of Uttar Pradesh (now Uttarakhand). District Dehradun has a very long history as far as industrial activities are concerned.

OLD-TIME INDUSTRIES

The production of woolen handloom has been an important industry of the district since early times. Koltas have traditionally been engaged in trade. Although the industry exists even today, it has considerably declined.

Tea plantations in Dehradun were started in 1840. By 1886 there were 33 tea gardens covering an area of 4,972 acres. The quality of Dehradun tea was considered among the best in the world. However, due to problems of change in climate, marketing and unwise management the potential for tea cultivation in Doon Valley was not realized in a sustained manner. In the post independence era the increasing urbanistion and institutional growth led to significant transfer of tea plantations to colonization needs of the advancing urban areas (Bandyopadhyay and Shiva, 1984). However, some small units still produce small quantity.

Capt. Hutton initiated the sericulture industry in the district in 1856. After some temporary set backs, the industry continued to prosper till 1880s. However, the output between the years 1898 and 1901 was poor. In 1898-99 sericulture was introduced in Jaunsar Bawar but the effort failed. The industry has been revived by the government efforts after independence and now stands on sound economic footing. At present, there are 26 mul-berry farms in the district covering an area of 246 acres and providing employment to about 3000 people.

The other old time industries of the district are the production of jaggery and of oil from oil seeds, manufacture of leather, pottery, handloom cloth, metal ware etc. After 1930, a number of industries of various magnitude have been established in the district. In 1951, 1961 and 1971 the number of registered units were 40, 45 and 358 respectively. According to an another estimate, by the end of 1970s Doon Valley had about 800 industrial units, small or big, including sugar, drugs, chemicals and textiles. Similarly, in 1972, two heavy industries– The Indian Drugs and Pharmaceuticals Ltd. and Sturdia Chemicals Ltd., seven large scale units and large number of small scale Industries and cottage and village industries were functioning.

In 1981, there were about 611 industrial units in Dehradun city alone. Out of them, 606 were small scale industries and the rest 5 heavy industries engaged in manufacturing of textile goods, electrical goods and chemical products. In addition, the city had a large number of small and unregistered units located all over the city.

In spite of these units, the district was not considered a developed one and was declared industrially backward in early 1980s. Under the backward area scheme, U.P. Government provided liberal finance to outside entrepreneurs for setting up mainly lime based industries such a cement, calcium carbide, calcium carbonate etc. District Industries Centre started functioning in 1978 to provide financial assistance, shed, power connection, raw material, marketing guidance etc. under one roof. In addition, U.P.F.C. and Garhwal Mandal Vikas Nigam also provided assistance to promote industrial tempo. For rapid growth, three sub-centres at Vikasnagar, Doiwala and Rishikesh were proposed. Out of which Vikasnagar and Rishikesh sub-centres have started functioning. Selakui and the nearby area in Sahaspur block was also identified as potential growth centers.

This way, during the post independence period till mid 1980s Dehradun had registered an impressive growth in industrial activities. In March 1989, district had 2703 registered industrial units, 2662 unregistered units and 76 units registered under Factory Act (PNB District Credit Plan 1989-90). Thus, the district is gifted not only with village and cottage industries and small scale industries but also with a number of large scale and heavy industries.

The utilization of mineral resources, predominantly high grade limestone, has been an old and significant economic activity in the Doon Valley. After independence, due to high quality and ready demand (in industries like steel, sugar, textiles, chemicals, glass etc.) lime-stone quarrying became a major activity of the Doon Valley. During the seventies and the early eighties there was a considerable increase in the establishment of lime based industries in and around Dehradun. Three extensive (hazardous and obnoxious) industries were established on the Mussoorie bye pass. These were namely, Uttar Pradesh Cement Corporation's Calcium Carbide Factory, RC Cement Factory and Aditya Chemicals. In addition, unabated mining and quarrying operations in Mussoorie foot hills as well as Sahasradhara area gradually led to a depletion of forests and deterioration of overall environment.

Dehradun city and its surrounding areas within a short span of time started facing a number of problems related to uncontrolled and haphazard development, traffic and transportation, proliferation of slums on the lowlands and at the beds of seasonal streams. Lime kilns, especially chemical industries proved the greatest nuisance. The air and dust pollution caused by these kilns also proved detrimental to human life as well as vegetation. The lime kilns which are located amidst the fertile agricultural land have rendered the soil unfertile besides creating serious problem of environmental pollution. In view of the rapidly changing physical and socio-economic profile of Doon Valley, the environmentalists pointed out: "Removal of limestone through the entire base of Mussoorie has led to severe destabilization of hill station. The Mall has been sinking, buildings are developing cracks, and support walls are collapsing. Mussoorie is being turned into a house without foundations ... quarrying in the Mussoorie hills has undermined the resource base for sustainable economic development through agriculture, horticulture, animal husbandry, tourism and the knowledge industry..... Besides affecting the water resources, quarrying in Doon Valley has also been responsible for destruction of agricultural land. Quarries and debris have significantly reduced the grazing areas available to the local people. This has led to a great decline, sometimes as much as 40 per cent in the cattle population, and similar loss in milk production" (Bandyopadhyay and Shiva, 1984). "Every tree that is felled now ultimately damages the life-support system–the soil water and the climate of the Indo-Gangetic Plain" (India Today 1986).

In order to check the haphazard development degradation of natural environment the state government notified "Mussoorie Dehradun Development Area" under the provisions of U.P. Urban Planning and Development Act, 1973 and also constituted "Musoorie Dehradun Development Authority" for the purpose of planning and development vide notification, dated 29.10.1984. Under the orders of the Supreme Court of India, most of the mines closed down in 1986.

Doon Valley Board recommended that the Doon Valley be declared an "environmentally fragile zone" and strict control be imposed over the location of new industries as the pressure of population and industries in the Doon Valley is creating serious problems of air, dust and water pollution. Keeping in view all these factors, the Expert Working Group constituted by the Department of Environment, Government of India, for review of Dehradun Master Plan, has recommended that land use for industries should not exceed 5 per cent of the total urbanisable area of Doon Valley. Accordingly, about 35 hectares (4.97 per cent of urbanisable area in 2002) has been earmarked for industrial use including the area under existing industries (M.D.D.A. Master Plan).

Conforming to the above steps, Department of Environment has also imposed some strict restrictions on industrial activities in the Doon Valley. All industries have been classified into three broad categories– (1) Green, (2) Orange, and (3) Red. Only Green industries have been allowed in Doon Valley subject to the following conditions :

1. All new industries will be permitted in approved industrial area only.
2. All new industries are required to obtain "No Objection Certificate" from U.P. Pollution Control Board.

The above steps have naturally adversely affected the industrial activities of the district and consequently all developmental activities have come to a gradual stagnation. It is evident from the number of industries which have not recorded any increase since 1989 (Table 1).

On the other hand, as a natural consequence of slow industrial development, the problem of unemployment has taken a serious turn. Employment is an urgent need in itself. Jobs alone can be the vehicle for raising the standard of living of the common man.

NEED FOR A REGIONAL POLICY

The importance of industrialization as a means for achieving rapid growth and prosperity has all along been recognized. Hence, present situation demands that we must develop, as early as a possible, a growth oriented regional industrial policy for Doon Valley to generate higher industrial potential, to modernize agriculture, to create more employment avenues, to encourage crafts and cottage industries based on locally available raw materials, to impart technical and vocational training to both men and women, and to evolve an effective marketing system. Preservation of environment is a good thing but development of economic activities is also a must for our survival. If our basic existence is endangered, who will use the resources? Thus, we should be prepared to pay some price for development. While developing such policy following points deserve serious considerations:

1. Local needs and resources be accorded top prioirity in selection of industries and all concerned authorities must extend their full co-opeation and support.
2. As far as possible eco-friendly resource based industries be given top priority. Pollution free industries like Traditional wool based handicraft industries, sericulture, electronics, engineering, handicrafts etc be given all possible support.
3. Food processing industries like preservation of fruits and vegetables have very bright future. Apple and potatoes can be used in varieties of ways.These industries can be very well established in and around Chakrata.

Table 1
Industries of Dehradun

	March 1980	March 1983	March 1986	March 1989	March 1990	March 1991	March 1992	March 1993	March 1994
Large/Medium Scale Industries			14	19					
No. of Small Scale Industries			872						
Registered Units	536	1009		2708	2708	2708	2708	2708	2708
Unregistered Units	1150	97		2662	2662	2662	2662	2662	2662
No. of Units Registered Under Factory Act	74	97		76	76	76	76	76	76
Some important Cottage/Village/Household Industries									
1. No. of handlooms				11	11	11	11	11	11
2. No. of Silk textiles units (Spinning and Weaving)				7	7	7	7	7	7
3. No. of Cotton Spinning/ Weaving units				18	18	18	18	18	18
4. No. of Khadi Units				392	392	392	392	392	392
5. No. of Shoe making/ leather works				410	410	410	410	410	410
6. No. of Village Pottery Units				150	150	150	150	150	150
7. No. of Hand made paper units				3	3	3	3	3	3
8. No. of Household processing units.				20	20	20	20	20	20
9. No. of Toy making units.				10	10	10	10	10	10
10. No. of other Handicrafts				50	50	50	50	50	50
11. No. of other Industries				1260	1260	1260	1260	1260	1260

Source(s) : Punjab National Bank: District Credit Plan– Dehradun 1980-82 and 1983-85.
Annual Action Plan– Dehradun 1986.
District Credit Plan– Dehradun 1989-90, 1990-91, 1991-92, 1992-93, 1993-94 and 1994-95.

4. Cold storages can also be further expanded in and around Dehradun and Rishikesh. Even today a fair portion of many fruits and vegetables perish in warm weather in the absence of sufficient and proper facilities.
5. Small scale industries based on wind and solar power can also be developed.
6. Tourism industry has a great potential. Dehradun is endowed with immense potentialities to be a place of great tourist attraction.
7. Tea industry has a glorious past. It can have a bright future as well. Efforts be made to revive this industry. If wisely managed and proper marketing is done, this industry can be revived on sound economic footing.
8. Among other industries activated carbon (produced from husk of rice) plaster of paris (manufactured from gypsum), hard-board, wood work, horticulture, fish culture, dairy, poultry farming, paper and pulp industry, carpet, pushmina shawls, namadas and some mineral based industries etc. can be properly organised. We may specially try to develop those traditional industries on modern lines which were quite prosperous in the past.

In addition, all industries included in the Green category, if properly developed on scientific basis can very well prove to be a boon to the economy of Doon Valley. Some relaxation is also possible. Hence, what is needed today is bold initiative and determined effort on our part to put Doon Valley on the industrial map of India.

NOTES

1. Owing to physiographic controls, the hinterland of Dehradun coincides more or less with the limits of Doon Valley.
2. According to Composite Index of industrial development (on the basis of 7 indicators) in 1970-71 Dehradun was placed in the category of 'Medium High' (value of composite index 0.7846) but in 1980-81 it moved to the category of 'High' (with the value of composite index 1.7862).

3. Criticising the move Bandhopadhyay and Shiva have observed that "the existence of the diverse and intensive industrial component of economic activity was completely overlooked when in early 1980s the district of Dehradun was declared "Industrially backward"..... The declaration of Dehradun as a "backward" district falsifies its industrial status, its high literacy status, and its developed agricultural and economic status.
4. Among Green industries all such non-obnoxious and non-hazardous industries have been included, which employ upto 100 persons and which do not use fuel in their manufacturing process or in any subsidiary process which does not emit toxic emissions of a diffused nature.

REFERENCES

Bandyopadhyay, J., and Shiva, Vandana (1984), Planning for Underdevelopment: The Case of Doon Valley, *Economic and Political Weekly*, January 28, Vol. 19, No. 4.

Badhwar, Inderjit, (Editor) (1986), Garhwal Himalayas: Plunder in the Hills, *India Today*, August 15.

Murray, D.B. (1960), *Industrial Development, A Guide for Accelerating Economic Growth*, New York, McGraw Hill Book Company, p. 3.

Punjab National Bank, District Credit Plan: Dehradun 1980-82, 1983-85. Annual Action Plan (1986) Dehradun, District Credit Plan: Dehradun 1989-90, 1990-91, 1991-92, 1992-93, 1993-94 and 1994-95.

Tewari, R.T. (1984), *Changing Patterns of Development in India*, New Delhi, Ashish Publishing House, p. 47, and 72.

Town and Country Planning Department, 1985, *Master Plan for Dehradun* 1982-2001, Lucknow, Government of U.P.

Varun, D.P. (1979), Uttar Pradesh District Gazetteers: Dehradun; Lucknow, Government of U.P., pp. 131-42.

10

MARRIAGE SYSTEM AMONG THE MUSLIMS OF DEHRADUN CITY

Zeinab Rahman

Dehradun is a beautiful city with an intellectual and peaceful ambience. Although Dehradun is a small city, it is very well developed and highly cosmopolitan in nature, as compared with other Indian cities of its size and population. This is shown by comparing various development indicators. People belonging to different religious and cultural backgrounds have made Dehradun their home and live here in peace and friendship. The various Central Govt. offices situated here are an important factor responsible for the concentration of educated and technically qualified people from all over the country. This, coupled with the excellent educational institutions operating in Dehradun, accounts for high literacy rate.

Muslims constitute about 8 per cent of the city's population. Of these, a greater number belong to lower S E S. Among the smaller number belonging to higher S E S, a few are very rich, majority being of middle class. Nearly half of the Muslims in Dehradun do not belong originally to this place instead they have migrated either in previous or present generation, mostly from the other parts of U P, but some have also migrated from eastern, central and southern states of India. This composite nature of the local Muslim community is responsible for its varied and heterogeneous culture; since Muslims from different regions interact a lot and learn various traits and habits from each other. They not only learn and share each other's cultural traits but they have also adopted many customs and habits from non-Muslims too, which they found convenient and beneficial. For instance, many Muslims in Dehradun do not eat meat everyday, instead have learnt to prepare a variety of vegetarian dishes from their non-Muslim friends. This culture is still evolving and less compared to the rigid deep-rooted culture of historically Muslim dominated places like Lucknow, Rampur, Bhopal or Hyderabad. Secondly, it is more amenable to change and has incorporated many new and liberal attributes. Here, migrants from different places have given up some of the ancient customs and traditions of their native places which they find cumbersome or incompatible with modern times. Only those customs, traditions and practices have been generally retained which are relevant or which can be modified and made relevant. In this way, the Muslim culture in Dehradun is comparatively more modern and liberal as proved by the research findings. For instance, in the sample from Derhadun, only 19.5 per cent respondents were not favourable to gainful employment of women while Indu Menon, in her study status of Muslim women in India (1981) writes, 65 per cent of our respondents feel that women should stay at home and perform the role of mother and wife only, rather than working outside. In Dehradun sample a majority of respondents were in favour of modern concepts like small family norm, practices of family planning, equal status of women in modern society, monogamy, similar treatment of sons and daughters with regard to education and so on.

An important constituent of the cultural aspect of any community is the institution of marriage. Marriage is a very basic and important social institution of a community. Among Muslims too, it is considered not only important but also essential, for both men and women. Marriage is also looked upon as a *Sunna* (practice of the Prophet) and therefore is regarded as obligation which must be fulfilled. (Lambat, 1976).

Muslim marriage is a civil contract and its only essential ceremony is *Nikah*, which is an announcement of both the bride and the groom's desire to become husband and wife at a fixed *Mehr* in front of two witnesses. The bridegroom hosts a dinner soon after to celebrate the occasion and this is known as *Walima*. *Nikah* is the actual marriage ceremony, mentioned and explained in Quran, while *Walima* is a *Sunna*. The prophet's daughter, Fatima was married in a very simple way, the only ceremonies being *Nikah* and *Walima*. This marriage is considered as an ideal form as prescribed in religious code. But in practice many customs and traditions which have no religious significance have got incorporated in the marriage ceremony everywhere, their character being regional. We might say that while *Nikah* and *Walima* fall in the category of great tradition, the various customs like *Sehra Bandi, Mehndi, Aarsi–Mashaf* etc. fall in the category of little tradition. Therefore in any Muslim community, whether Indian or Arabian, marriage is celebrated according to the prevalent customs and traditions, besides performing the essential ceremonies, like *Nikah*. The most prevalent procedure is considered the accepted and traditional procedure.

Marriage in Dehradun is celebrated mostly in the traditional style, but research findings show that as compared to the older generation, more marriages are being celebrated in a modern style among the younger generation. It has also been found that many changes in the form of traditional marriage itself, have been introduced and accepted by the community. An emphasis on this aspect of Muslim in Dehradun, will show that Dehradun Muslims are comparatively more modern and amenable to change than most other Indian Muslims.

The first step in marriage is the selection of marriage partner. Traditionally this job was performed solely by parents. The parents or elders of the boy searched for a suitable girl, mostly among close relatives or among distant relative and sometimes among close friends. The caste factor was considered very important, so that the Syeds wanted to marry only among the Syeds whereas other Ashraf castes generally inter-married. Other important factors that were taken into consideration included the socio-economic status of the family, the education, occupation, salary and looks in case of a boy; and good looks, household skills and a pleasant nature in case of girl. The boy and girl to be married were not consulted, just informed. All this has changed to a great extent in the Muslim community in Dehradun. Data show that more than half the respondents said that caste is not at all a factor in selection of marriage partner, it is enough if the family is Muslim; only about one fourth respondents said that caste is still an important factor, in order to maintain purity of descent. Another important change is that parents have started consulting their children, both, sons and quite often daughters too, before fixing their marriages. In fact, in many cases parents agree with their children's choice in selection of marriage partner. Although a great majority were in favour of arranged marriages, i.e. arranged by parents, almost all of them agreed that the children should be consulted and their wishes should be acknowledged. Only a negligible number differentiated between sons and daughters by saying, in case of a girl, her opinion need not be taken. A third of the respondents held the modern and liberal view that in modern times, educated youngsters can choose good life partners without parental advice. Education is becoming an increasingly important factor in mate selection, not only for boys but also for girls, in both rich and middle class families. The latest favourable attribute for a girl in modern, educated families is, a good job. There is a great demand for girls who are doctors, lecturers or Govt. employees.

Once the boy's parents decide about a suitable match, they pay a visit to the house of the prospective bride, to make the proposal. After a couple of visits and some enquiries, the proposal is accepted by the bride's parents. Traditionally, the bride's parents deemed it seemly to take a long time in giving their approval, but now a days, when good matches are difficult to find, parents of daughters are becoming more practical and welcoming good matches openly. Sometimes the girl's parents, indirectly, inform the boy's parents that a proposal for their daughter is welcome. This also is an instance of giving up customs which are not worthwhile in modern times.

When the proposal is accepted, formal announcement is made at the engagement ceremony, when some close relatives and friends of both sides are invited to the bride's house. The bride-groom's mother presents a set of clothes and a piece of jewellery, often a ring, to the bride. Sweets and fruits are also presented. The bride's parents host a dinner or high tea for all the guests. Some people have a custom of performing a similar ceremony at the boy's place after a couple of days. Others perform both ceremonies simultaneously at the bride's house. Generally the date of marriage is also fixed on that day. Most people prefer short engagements, unless there is some particular reason for delaying. Some modern families who do not like elaborate ceremonies, just fix the marriage date once a suitable matche is found.

An important marriage ceremony, of pan-Indian character, with some regional variations, is *Mayun*. It is performed two or four days before the actual wedding. In Dehradun, in this ceremony the bride takes a ceremonial bath. A paste of turmeric, sandalwood powder and other ingredients is applied to her. This paste is called *Ubtan*, and is considered effective for making the skin smooth and fair. She is made to wear yellow clothes and all the guests too prefer wearing shades of yellow. Certain rites are performed by married women. Earlier, close relatives used to have fun smearing each other with *Ubtan*; but these days it is restricted to applying a little on the cheek or chin of those performing the rites of garlanding the bride. This is another example of giving up a messy and sometimes unpleasant, custom. Traditionally, songs suitable for the occasion are sung by womenfolk. Some people organize a *Milad*, too, in which religious verses are recited. The changes in this ceremony include a secular type of 'Ladies Sangeet' with songs and dances from films, in place of traditional songs. Generally, a few religious and auspicious songs are sung first, followed by latest songs etc. The guests are served snacks or food at the end of the ceremony.

These days another ceremony, called *Mehndi*, is being performed with a lot of fanfare. The local people say that this ceremony has been adopted by those who have visited Pakistan to attend marriages, or have many relatives there, because this ceremony is popular in Pakistan. Actually this ceremony is performed with great pomp and splendour in some parts of India, since ages. For instance, it is a very important and interesting ceremony among Muslims of Hyderabad, the capital of Andhra Pradesh. Thus *Mehndi* ceremony is a regional phenomenon which has been adopted by Muslims of Dehradun, because it is interesting and gorgeous.

In the *Mehndi* ceremony the bride's sisters and other young female relatives deck themselves and carry decorated plates of *Mehndi, Ubtan* and flowers, besides a set of clothes, shoes, other accessories for the groom and sweets, to the groom's house. This ceremony is performed one day before the marriage. At the groom's place the bride's sister applies *Mehndi* to the groom's finger, amidst joking and laughter. The groom gives a certain amount of money to his would be sisters-in-law, after *Mehndi* is applied. This money is known as *Neg*. Girls from both sides sing songs, mainly to tease one another. The guests are served sweets and drinks before leaving.

The traditional Muslim marriage in Dehradun is usually solemnised during the day time. If the bride groom's party is local and it suits both parties, then *Nikah* may be performed in the evening.

On the marriage day, the relatives gather in the bride groom's house much before the marriage party, known as the *Barat*, is scheduled to start for the venue of marriage. The groom gets ready and is blessed by his elders. Then his sisters tie the *Sehra* to his forehead in the presence of all the relatives. The *Sehra* is made of flowers and the ceremony is known as *Sehra Bandi*. After this, the groom leaves for the bride's house together with his male relatives and friends. This cavalcade is the *Barat*. Earlier, female relatives did not go with the *Barat*, or only a few went; but now all female relatives accompany the

Barat, in cars or bus. This is one instance where women have been given more freedom and a greater role to play in modern times, as compared with the past.

At the bride's house the *Barat* is received in a befitting manner, with garlands, sweets and drinks. These days many people prefer to perform the marriage at a marriage hall, rather than at home, since it is more convenient. This again is a departure from tradition. One reason for this is, that now a days reception of *Barat* and dinner are done on grand scale, involving hundreds of guests of different background, and not only relatives; therefore a bigger and better organized venue like a marriage hall or a hotel is more suitable. Once the bride is ready; many fashionable brides go to beauty parlours for this; she is taken to the marriage hall. All others are already there. When the *Barat* is received and the *Quazi* arrives, then *Nikah* is performed. Generally seating arrangements are made separately for men and women. The region for males is called the *Mardana* and for females, the *Zanana*. *Nikah* is the essential ceremony of Muslim marriage. In the male gathering, the *Quazi* delivers a discourse of desirability and importance of marriage and also on the rights and obligations of husband and wife. Then he performs the *Nikah* after confirming the consent of both the bride and groom in the presence of witnesses. These witnesses are generally close male relatives of the bride. The *Mehr* is fixed and accepted by both parties. The signature of the groom, the bride and witnesses and also the *Quazi* are taken on the *Nikahnama* (marriage document). Then the *Nikah* is complete. People congratulate the groom, his parents and the bride's parents. Traditionally, the bride was expected to cover herself completely and neither speaks to anyone or look at anyone, so no question arose of congratulating her. But these days the brides, though they cover themselves and sit quietly, do talk softly to friends and sisters and some also are made to sit with the groom after *Nikah* so that all the guests can congratulate the couple. This practice is quite rare, though. Generally, the bride continues to sit in the *Zanana*, after *Nikah*. The groom's mother puts on some jewellery for the bride as symbols of married status, like the *Nath* (nose-ring) and *tika* (jewellery for forehead). Soon after the *Nikah,* dry food like almonds, dates, and *Misri* (sugar lumps) are distributed to all the guests from the groom's side. This is an old custom originating from Arabia. It is said that the Prophet had distributed dried dates to guests at his daughter's marriage. Traditionally these dry fruits are kept in big trays near the seat of the groom and soon after the *Nikah,* they are showered around him and those assembled, specially the youngsters scramble to collect as many as possible. The same is also done in the *Zanana.* These days may people prefer to distribute small packets of dry fruits to guests, while some have given up this custom.

After the *Nikah,* a sumptuous dinner is served to all the guests, in which *Pulao* or *Biryani* and *Kababs* are a must. There are other dishes including sweet dishes too. The next important ceremony, which is performed in many families in Dehradun, is *Aarsi-Mashaf.* In this ceremony the bride and groom are made to sit opposite each other and the groom is shown the bride's face in a mirror, placed between them. In the traditional families this is probably the first time the groom sees his bride.

The *Vidai* or *Rukhsati* is the next ceremony which literally means bidding farewell to the newly married daughter. The parents and close relatives bless the newly married couple and send them off to start a new life. Many minor ceremonies are performed at this time; for instance, some people have a custom of handing over the bride to the groom by the bride's father; people originating from eastern U.P. have the custom of the bride throwing some rice behind, in her father's courtyard, before leaving with her husband. This is a local custom in towns of eastern, U.P., regardless of religion.

At the groom's house the bride is received by her-in-laws. She is bedecked with jewellery and flowers and all the relatives come to see her and give her gifts. This ceremony is known as *Runumai* which literally means showing of the face. Some minor ceremonies are also performed in some families, like preparing 'kheer' for the bride and demanding of *Neg* by the groom's sisters and so on.

Traditionally, the next morning the bride's younger brothers and sisters go to the groom's house to bring the bride home. In the evening the groom and his people are invited for dinner. This dinner is known as *Chauthi*. Many people have given up this custom now; the reason being, too much expenditure and sometimes unpleasantness caused by the practical jokes which were part of the ceremony. This is another instance of giving up irrelevant customs. Some practical jokes like hiding the groom's shoes are now played of the wedding day itself. Earlier many other practical jokes were played with the groom, his sisters, mother etc. Women on either side throw flowers and even vegetables on each other for fun. Verbal jokes and teasing sometimes lead to heated arguments. Thus it appears to be a positive step to give up this ceremony, while at the same time incorporating the harmless fun in the wedding itself.

The last important marriage ceremony is the *walima* dinner. This is hosted by the bride groom's parents a couple of days or a week after the marriage. Relatives on both sides are invited, but the bride's relatives are the guests of honour. *Walima* is considered essential as it is a *Sunna*.

Research findings show that 92 per cent respondents said their marriage was performed in traditional style; half of whom said some ceremonies were performed i.e., the essential and some common and pan-Indian. About a fourth said many ceremonies were performed i.e., mostly essential ones only. In the younger generation, i.e., the children of the respondents, 60 are married and of these 60 marriages only 61 per cent were performed in traditional style; while the percentage of mixed style and modern style marriages was higher in the younger generation as compared to the older generation. Most of the 61 per cent traditional marriages were performed with some ceremonies and about a fifth were performed with many ceremonies.

All this shows that in a generation's time changes have taken place in the marriage style of Muslims of Dehradun, towards modernity. Other changes in the institution of marriage were found to be as follows: increase in marriage

age for girls, simplification and secularization of elaborate ceremonies, change in pattern of expenditure as earlier more money was spent on hospitality while now more is spent on clothes, jewellary, decoration, photos and general show. This is the reason why great expenditure is incurred even at a son's wedding these days.

Change is an essential element of life and every group or community is always undergoing some change or the other. Processes of change, while tending to change the social system, may actually be helping to maintain it; because a social system needs to adapt itself to new circumstances in order to survive. Thus change and continuity are closely related. The above discussion of Muslim marriage in Dehradun shows how change and continuity go hand in hand. After enumerating the changes, one has to consider the factors that are responsible for the change. Some important factors of change in contemporary Indian society are industrialization, urbanization, spread of education, improvement in communication methods, new technology, new laws and new ideology. All these factors are operating in Dehradun too, and have influenced the Muslims of the city also. But certain factors have had a greater influence on the Muslims than others. For instance industrialization and urbanization, although they have brought about various changes like change in occupation, income and life style of many people., have not had as great an impact on Muslims of Dehradun as spread of education or improvement in mass media. Research findings show that only 10.5 per cent respondents are illiterate and a majority of the literate is educated up to high school or above. In all liberal and modern views expressed, a great number of respondents were educated upto or above high school. Some illiterate or little educated respondents also expressed liberal views and it was found that the factors responsible here were exposure to mass media, like television, and contact with people of diverse background. The last mentioned factor, inter-action with people of different regions, religions and cultures, was found to be very important in bringing about social change among all Muslims of the sample. For instances, those respondents who have friends belonging to all religions were found to have changed much more than those who have only Muslim friends, since the last decade, in various aspects of their lives.

Thus the Muslim of Dehradun are evolving a composite culture in which we find a blend of continuity and change, of tradition and modernity, and this is seen in their marriage procedure too. Education, exposure to mass media and interaction with different social groups have helped the Muslims to accept change and benefit through it, by adopting new practices which are compatible with modern times. With this, of course, they are maintaining all those cultural attributes which are exclusive to them and do not hinder their progress. Thus their culture is a unique mixture of the old and the new.

11

DOON'S JHANDA SAHIB

Gauri Shanker Bhatt & H. N. Mishra

The growing multitude of tourists, touching Dehradun every summer, hardly get aware that this city of inspiring scenic beauty and lovely picnic spots, scattered all around, owes its origin to a stride of India's political history and to a panthic schism which was more political than religious.

THE BACKDROP

It began in the year 1661 AD. After consolidating his hold on the Mughal throne, Aurangzeb summoned Har Rai, the seventh Guru of the Sikh, to Delhi. Realising the criticalness of the summon, his eldest son, Ram Rai, offered to visit Delhi as his father's emissary. As recorded by historians, by his wisdom, presence of mind, scholarship and miraculous spiritual power, he could establish a happy liason with the emperor. But, in spite of that, he lost in the succession to gurudom, to the seat of ecclesiastical-political power.

When Delhi became politically hot for Ram Rai, Aurangazeb is said to have refrained him from meddling in politics and sent him to the quiet oblivion of the Doon. With a firman from Aurangzab in the name of the then ruler of Garhwal, Fatah Shah, and moving along the upstream of Yamuna, Ram Rai entered Doon in 1675 AD. After having encamped for some time at the village Kandli, on the southern bank of the river Tons, he shifted to village Khurbura, now a mohalla of Dehradun.

For, Khurbura, along with six other villages–Rajpur, Chamasari, Dhamawala, Dhurtawala, Kanwali and Panditwari–formed his jagir, bestowed upon him by the Raja of Garhwal. Most of these villages have now been engulfed, as mohalles, in the swelling urban conglomerate at Dehradun. Guru ka Bag and chabutra (raised platform) are the only remains of Ram Rai's association with the village Kandli, now a part of Dehradun's cantonment. Near Khurbura, in what is now Jhanda Mohalla. Ram Rai planted and unfurled his flag, establishing as jagirdar and religious leader (Guru) of a section of Udasi Panth. There, after his demise (1687), was built his dehra (mausoleum) and the present gurudwara. In due course, in the four corners of his dehra, were built the dehras of his four wives.

Today, in the vicinity of Doon's railway station, stands a fortress like structure with its outshining minarets and domes, Dehras of Ram Rai and his wives, his residence, the gurudwara and the residence of its mahant (the head)–now ninth in succession–are housed inside this building. Built in Mughal style and decorated with beautiful but decaying frescoes, this complex is known as Darbar Shri Guru Ram Rai, popularly abbreviated as Darbar Sahib. In front of the imposing gate for this building, glitter in the sky, about one hundred feet high flag, at the place where Guru Ram Rai first planted it. This is the Jhanda Sahib, the symbol of Darbar's authority, of spiritual power of its founder and of religious compassion and pluralism. It has been Dehradun of today.

EMERGENCE OF DEHRA

In the late 16th and early 17th centuries, when one Rani Karnavati is said to have governed the valley, there was the Doon but not Dehradun. Some of the villages–Kaulagarh, Karanpur and Rajpur which formed a part of her domain, are now merged in the urban complex of Dehradun. Interestingly, what is the Doon to the sophisticated English-educated gentry, it just Dehra to the ruralities of Garhwal and early immigrants to the city. In the early records of the British Raj, it is Dehra and not Dehradun.

The term Doon is a common noun, meaning levelled land (wide valley) lying in between two mountains. That is why, Garhwal has many doons, particularized as Parwadoon, Pachwadoon and the famous tourists spot, Har Ki Doon. In the later part of the British Raj, when the valley opened up after the establishment (1820) of the hill station at Mussoorie and tea estates and extension of railway line to *Dehra*, as it seems, doon was suffixed to *Dehra* to particularize reference to the city of Dehradun. Derivatively speaking, Dehradun stands for the Doon which is identified by the Dehra(s).

When the British entered the valley as allies of the Raja of Garhwal and annexed it from the Gurkhas (1817) its population numbered 2100 with 500 dwellings. The British were politically interested in the valley to have unobstructed access to the strategic passes of niti and mana to contain Tibetans. They, however, developed it as a holiday resort. For, in its cool murfereshing air, they could feel a breath of their home climate. Consequently, it became a star attraction for the retired, being known as 'the city of green hedges and gray hair', which have been disappearing fast over the last three decades.

In its early phase, it was surrounded by sprawling, lush-green tea estates, many of which have now been devoured by urbanization and many have since disappeared. Commodious and imposing mansions, set in the midst of spacious and thick *lichi* gardens, are now developing into posh slums of cement and concrete, inhabited by the urban middle class, mostly drawn from neuveaux riches. Dehradun became famous for its *basmati* rice the demand for which is now far greater than its supply.

Today, its once green and wooded surrounding hills are sieved with lime-stone quarries, the working of which has now been legally banned. A vast majority of its *lichi*-gardens now exist but only in the records of the government. Its periphery is now dotted with lime-kilns, emitting dark, grey clouds of smoke in the atmosphere. It is now more known for its lime-stone and lime, small scale industries of miniature bulbs and

Tibetan carpets and potato, ginger and turmeric grown in the deep recesses of surrounding mountains.

The Dehradun of today is a sprawling city of five lac rather a semi-industrial town, set in the social matrix of a cosmopolitan middle class, drawn from all over the country. It is mostly employed in or retired from the offices of Government of India and scientific and educational institutions for which the city is well-known in India and abroad. Having elitist and aristocratic origin, the city has tended to retain a cultural hiatus between the upper and the lower. Its upper class is more European than the European. And, above all, it has attained the fame of what is now naught- *woh Dehradun ab Kahan* (that Dehradun is no more). In this romantic and painful longing lies the ethos of Dehradun, a hope for tomorrow.

DARBAR SAHIB

Dehradun has grown along with and in spite of the tradition of *Darbar Shri Guri Ram Rai*. The organic relationship between Darbar and Dehradun weakened after stimulating city's early urbanization. The *Jhanda* cult and its annual fortnightly fair are intrinsic to Doon's ruralistic culture. The panthic schism, to which Dehradun owes its origin, grew differently in Dehra's synthesizing social climates.

Ram Rai's youngest wife, who managed the jagir after his demise decreed that the *mehant* (*head*) of the *Darbar,* would henceforth be a celebrate and nominee of the *mahant* in office, *sajjade nashin*. From the *Darbar* has spread the message of equality between man and man, divided by caste, creed, colour and station in life. All paths lead to the God as rivers lead to the sea. Accordingly, compassion of the God falls equally on all provided there is required devotion towards that formless and ominipresent power, revealing itself in the ways demonstrated by the *Guru*. This is the cardinal tenet of *bhaktism,* rather ideological mainstay of the silent revolution which shook India's psyche in the fading twilight of Mughal power but was disturbed and arrested by the political ascendancy of the British.

The Darbar, however, has had its following in Punjab (Samrala, Patiala, Ropar, Hoshiarpur, Jalandhar, Kiratpur, Anandpur Sahib and Nangal), Haryana (Ambala, Jagadhari and Yamuna Nagar) and western Uttar Pradesh (Bijnor, Moradabad, Beroilly, Itawa, Mathura, Buland Shahar and Meerut). After partition, Delhi has grown into a stronghold of its adherents. Some of its followers have settled abroad as well. The Darbar drew its followers both from high and low but, as said, mostly from the lower rungs of India's traditional hierarchical social structure.

Dehra's civic and social life once revolved round the *Darbar*, cast in the feudalistic style of the time. The mahant functioned and lived like a feudal with feudal peraphernelia. Like a benevolent feudal, he helped the needy and the poor in marriage and exigencies of life. He provided help and shelter to immigrants and refugees to the city. To be allowed to use *Darbar's* bagghi, horse driven carriage, in marriage procession, was till recently a symbol of social prestige. With free accommodation and messing provided by the *Darbar*, many a youngmen could receive education and improve their prospects in life.

The city has grown mostly on the land once owned by the *Darbar*. Yet, the growth of city gradually reduced *Darbar's* importance in Dehra's social-political life. The *Darbar*, too, has gradually been shaking off the traditional symbols of feudal glory. The tradition of the *mahant* driving in procession in a horse-driven carriage with glittering umbrella and attendant retenue and the herald (*chobdar*) has now gone into the oblivion of oral history. Shri Guru Ram Rai college at Dehradun, imparting education upto post-gradaute classes, and thirty two schools–out of which nineteen are English medium public schools–located in Punjab, Haryana and Garhwal, run and managed by the *Darbar*, today, tell a different tale.

JHANDA MELA

Doon's *Jhanda Mela*, a part of Darbar's *Jhanda* cult, has grown into a cultural tradition of the city. A fornightly annual event, it ceremonially begins with the flag-hoisting ceremony, held on the fifth of the blackfortnight of the month of *Chaitra* (March). It is celebrated as birth anniversary of Darbar's founder. It is said to have been started in his life time.

It is an occasion of mass-affirmation of the solidarity of panthic brotherhood, allegiance to Darbar's temporal authority and belief in the ritual beneficence of the Guru's spiritual power, symbolized in the *Jhanda Sahib*. In this affirmation, *sangat* (ceremonial gathering of panthic brotherhood), particularly the *sangat* from Punjab, occupies the importance of socio-historical tradition.

With the dispatch of *hukumnama* (the letter of order), through a messenger of the Darbar, in the name of subordinate mahant of Bahlolpur (Kharar tehsil, near Chandigarh), starts the process of *Jhanda* ceremony. The *hukumnama* contains the date and day of the ceremony and invitation to lead the *sangat* for occasion. Accordingly, the *sangat* ceremonially starts from Bahlolpur. Halting at Badegaon, Gopal Mochan and Khijrabad, the *sangat* reaches Raiyanwala eight days before the date of *Jhanda* ceremony.

All these villages lie in the Ambala district of Haryana. Raiyanwala, an important link in the ceremony, lies across Yamuna, at a distance of about fortytwo kilometers from Dehradun. As per tradition, at Raiyanwala, the *mahant* accords a ceremonial welcome to the *sangat*. Colourfully dressed men and women–*the sangat* with their luggage on their heads, shoulders and bicycles and accompanied by trumpetters slowly move towards Raiyanwala. In the green-yellow aura, radiating from half-ripened crops and greenery of nature, and in the backdrop of Siwalik Hills, the villagers of Raiyanwala and surroundings villages trail in single files, along zigzag paths, to join the *sangat*. The crowd presents the spectacle of a small colourful village *mela*.

The *sangat* has to reach Raiyanwala before the arrival of the *Mahant*. On the same day, in the morning, starts *Mahant's* procession from Dehradun. Accompanied by his attendants and retinue, the procession of the *Mahant* now travels in a bus owned by the *Darbar*. The villagers of Timli and Rampur welcome the procession by paying their obeisance to the

Mahant. As a gesture of gratitude, sweets and small coins are distributed among children on behalf of the *Darbar*.

Members of the *sangat* welcome the *Mahant* at Raiyanwala by paying their obeisance to him and presenting him with flowers, money (coins and notes) and, in some cases, with the pieces of silver and gold ornaments. The *sangat* is fed after the ceremony of hoisting Guru's flag.

As goes the oral tradition, three hundred years ago, Guru Ram Rai is said to have hoisted his flag here before entering the Doon. The flag-hoisting ritual at Raiyanwala commemorates that event. The very name Raiyanwala suggests that the village might have been founded by Ram Rai.

In the afternoon, after tea and snacks have been served to the *sangat*, *Mahant* returns to *Darbar*. The *sangat* follows on foot. It is received next at Sahaspur and, then, at Kanwali, a village situated at a distance of about three kilometers from the Darbar and fighting losing battle with urban invasion from Dehra. To receive the *sangat* at Kanwali, the *Mahant*, in procession, walks all the way from Darbar to Kanwali. From there, he leads the *sangat* to *Darbar* through Darshani Gate–the gate from where a full view of Guru's *samadhi* (shrine) can be had. After paying obeisance at the shrine, the *sangat* goes round the *mausolaum* (parikrama).

The *sangat* is then accommodated in tents, put up for the purpose, and in the corridors and rooms of the gurudwara. The *langar* (public kitchen) provides food to the *sangat* which reaches Darbar six days before the scheduled day of ceremony. In the meantime, its number keeps on swelling with the followers of the Darbar gradually moving in from surroundings. It reaches its maximum number in the early hours of the morning of the day of Jhanda ceremony.

In the Darbar, members of the *sangat* celebrate the festival of colour (Holi). To pay obeisance at the shrine of the Guru, to have audience with the *Mahant*, to seek his blessings and to spend time in singing devotional songs (*bhajan*) and in meditation becomes daily ritual of the members of the *sangat* till arrival of the day of grand ritual, colloquially known as *Jhanda charhana* (flag hoisting).

With the help of ropes, ladders and supporting poles, the flag and its mast are brought down to the ground. The flag is then taken off. The huge covering of the mast is removed and carried to be dumped in a corner of Darbar's spacious courtyard. The mast is ritually changed every third year and is brought from the jungle of Dudhli which is now a part of Rajaji National Park. As far as possible, it is taken in one piece about a hundred feet long. And, if one piece is not available, two pieces may be joined together.

Members of the *sangat* consecrate the mast by bathing it with Ganga-water mixed with milk and smearing it with curd and the paste of sandalwood and turmeric. Around noon, members of the *sangat* collectively hold the mast shoulder-high for the clothing ceremony. The devotees offer to *Jhanda Sahib* long cylindrical coverings, open at both ends and mostly of white colour. Some of the men and women sit in rows stitching these coverings. Carrying devotee's name, they are queued in long rows. Previously, the mast was passed through each covering offered by the devotees. Now, since the number of the devotees has increased, the bundle of each covering is touched at one end of the mast and passed along to the other.

While these rituals are on, the devotees find time to pay homage to the shrine of the Guru and beg for his grace. There, dressed in the traditional long robe and conical cap, sit the Mahant blessing the devotees and receiving presents from them. To help in cooking and cleaning utensils of the langar and to have *prasad* (food) there, are religious obligations which almost every devotee performs happily.

In the later part of the afternoon, when the clothing ceremony is over, starts regal dressing and decoration of *Jhanda Sahib*. The mast is wrapped in yellow velvet. Over that is placed a covering of dark maroon valvet, brocaded with golden and silver laces. These coverings are provided by the *Darbar*. A little below the thinnest end of the mast, is tied a long triangular flag, maroon in colour. Towards the thick end of the mast are fastened/tied coloured handkerchiefs, mostly of bright red colour with glittering golden lining. Offered by the devotes, these handkerchiefs are given away as Prasad (favour).

As evening draws near, a big crowd gathers around the marbled pedestal of the flag, in the open spaces between the dried up pond and Darbar-building and on the surrounding housetops. The *Mahant*, then, gestures to the *sangat* to erect the flag. First raised by hands, and then, dragged by thick ropes and pushed up by hand-held poles, the thinner part of the mast gradually starts moving upwards. When raised a little more than halfway, the mast gets a higher momentum and gets set in the hole of its pedestal with a heavy thud. The crowd, looking at it spell-bound, suddenly breaks into the cries of *'Guru Ram Rai ki Jai'*, *'Jhanda Sahib ki Jai'*, *'Guru Govind Singh ki Jai'* and *'Guru Nank ki Jai'*.

At night, the *sangat* goes on *parikrama* (roams about) of what appears to be the original boundary of Dehra. From near the *Jhanda Sahib*, it moves to Bhandar Chowk, Ramlila Bazar, Hanuman Chowk, Darshani Gate, Baradari and back to *Jhanda Sahib*. On the third day, after the day of flag-hoisting, the *sangat*, led by the *Mahant*, goes on *nagar parikrama* (round the city). This *parikrama* starts from Darbar and covers Kanwali Road, Khurbura, Bindal Bridge, Chakrata Road, Ghantaghar, Gandhi Road, Gaughat, Bombay Bag and Lakkhi Bag.

The city of today has gone far beyond this traditional boundary of *nagar parikrama*. However, within the area of this *parikrama* are situated most of the local educational institutionas of the *Darbar*. In Lakkhibag are situated shrines of the late *mahants*, along with the old celebrated cremation ground of the city. In the morning of the day, following the day of *nagar parikrama*, the *sangat* is ceremonially seen off by the *Mahant*. Then follow the devotees from Haryana and Western Uttar Pradesh.

THEN AND NOW

Gone are the days, when the *sangat* came on foot in a large number and the *Mahant*, riding an elephant, led it all the way from Raiyanwala. Now, only a small party, rather a token of the *Sangat*, comes on foot. The *Mahant* now welcomes the *sangat* where it used to camp at night. They, as in the past, come with their families, combining religion and outing. With growing and improved means of transport, number of the *sangat* has tended to swell. But, easier and faster means of transport tend to render it transient as well.

As in the goneby days, *Jhanda Mela* is no more a cultural event of the entire community. It is also not a cultural event for the vulgarly westernized new rich, the Englilsh-educated and the recent middle class migrants to the city. It, however, continues to be a cultural event in the life of the commoner, the lowly placed, irrespective of their caste, creed and *desh* (linguistic region). This is evident in the performance of tonsure ceremony near and under the blessings of *Jhanda Sahib.* Villagers of the Doon and from foothills visit the *mela* to pray for the beneficent blessings of *Jhanda Sahib* and to make purchases of their requirements from the *mela* and/or from city's market.

Jhanda mela, as recalled by old timers, used to be a big market of *sarees,* cloth, earthenware, woodwork and other goods, not produced in the valley. The inhabitants of the valley and surrounding hills also used to bring their produce for exchange. Growing industrialization and rail-road transport and city's market have tended to reduce its importance as an institution of exchange and annual market.

In spite of urban growth, sale of earthenware still retains its old importance. However, the *mela* has now been reduced to small shops, mostly local, selling factory made goods particularly, plastic toys-glass bangles, artificial jewellery, cosmetics and other articles of women's personal paraphernalia. Carved wooden goods of Saharanpur and kitchenware of daily use and wooden toys for children are a good attraction. So are marry-go-rounds, now electrically driven, small circuses, cheap dance parties, bidi-advertisers and colourful studios of traveling photographers.

To visit *Jhanda Mela* is an annual affair in the family-life of an average Doonwala. The visit is partly religious and partly festive. What impresses most is the fact that almost everyone visiting *Jhanda Mela,* irrespective of his caste and creed, offers sweets, incense, flowers (prasad) to Jhanda Sahib and bows before it and at the shrine of Guru Ram Rai. This is a living example of secularism as we define it. In this pluralistic world-view lies the spirit of our emotional interaction which is now being marred by the politics of religion and Panth and language and region. Being in hurry, the growing multitude of tourists to the city, overlook this message of Dehra's legend.

12

BANNUWALS: A PROFILE OF AN IMMIGRANT POPULATION OF N.W.F.P.

Vatsala Sarkar

The Bannuwal as the name suggests are the people of the Bannu region of N.W.F.P. of the erstwhile undivided India, now a part of Pakistan. The term is said to have been derived from one Shetab and his wife Bannu, the founders of the Bannuchae tribe. The Hindu population of Bannu migrated from this place in the wake of the partition of the country which also marks the most turbulent times of the history of independence movement. Lakhs of people were brutally done to death and millions rendered homeless as a result of the communal frenzy which gripped the nation and spelt doom for millions of innocent people who had to flee in precarious circumstances with whatever little belonging they could, towards Indian side as North West provinces fell to the side of Pakistan.

It we look into the history of the N.W.F.P. under British rule it would be evident that the province had earned its reputation for notoriety, incidence of looting and arson, foreign invasion and tribal insurgency to the extent that even the mighty British Power felt helpless and had to relent in giving autonomy to these tribal areas under the charge of a political agent acting as a mediator between the two. The tribals, mostly of Afghan origin like Mahsuds, Afridis, Muhammadans, Khattaks, Marawats, Balluchies are scattered all over the province and constantly remained at warring heads with each other.

Towards the end of Afghan war in 1919 followed by the emergence of Khan Abdul Gaffar Khan, who founded the Khudai Kidmatgar Movement or the Red Shirt Movement, against the tyranious rule of the British, it became imminent that British would be leaving the country but not without exacting its price i.e., dividing the people on communal lines. Muhammad Ali Jinnah, the founder of the Muslim league made his intention apparent that Muslim would no longer remain content in a Hindu dominated state, so they wanted a separate homeland; Pakistan. The fate of N.W.F.P. remaining a part of India or going over to Pakistan was finally resolved through a refrendum on 3rd June 1947, and thus it became a part of Pakistan.

According to census report of 1911, the Hindu and Sikh population of Bannu was 20,721 and 3746 against the overwhelming majority of 2,22,374 Mulsim peasants. As a consequence of the terms of refrendum in the changed socio-political situation and amidst the growing feeling of communal intolerance, mistrust and hatred, a large scale exodus of Hindu population of these provinces who were in minority, began towards Indian territory.

Since Government had opened rehabilitation camps at different places for the immigrants, many Bannuwals came to be settled in Dehradun. As per a rough estimate there were 1000 households of Bannuwals at the time this study was conducted. They are mostly scattered in old localities of Dehradun namely, Premnagar, Patelnagar, Karanpur, Mannuganj, Machli Bazar, Motibazar and the like. Interestingly enough, a considerable population of Bannuwals continue to inhabit the army barracks located in Premnagar which were allotted to them by the Government at the time of their migration to this place.

Since Bannuwals are essentially a territorial group it is wrong to assume that they belong to one ethnic stock. There are thus amongst them Khatri Arora (69.57%), Bhatia (23.27%), Brahmin (2.67%), Dard (1.96%), Sikh (2.58%) and Nirankari (0.59%). These castes are endogamous but a lot of relaxation in caste rules governing connubiality and commonsality have been witnessed ever since partition and their subsequent settlement to this place.

There have been frequent intermarriages between the Arora Khatris and Bhatias despite the fact that the former claims a superior status in terms of caste hierarchy. Likewise there are frequent intermarriages between Hindus and Sikhs. While negotiating marriage, the first preference is obviously given to own caste but if not possible then they look for match with castes of similar status within Bannuwals. Now-a-days marriages take place with members belonging to different territorial groups of N.W.F.P. like Dera Gajikhan, Dera Ismailkhan and the like. Even marriages with local Khatris have been solemnized due to paucity of finding good prospective match within their own group. However, despite relaxation territorial affiliations play a dominant role in regulating interpersonal relationship. Interestingly there are not very many castes among the Bannuwals and notably there are no scheduled castes among them. It is argued that in Bannu, menial and impure professions were largely performed by the Muslims. Besides, the stigma attached to the low professions is not so pronounced.

Bannuwals prefer to maintain the joint family system despite the growing influence of urbanization and industrialization which favours the growth of nuclear families. The common Bannuwal household consists of parents and married children. The eldest male heads the household and has an overall control over the domestic expenditure. People feel that joint family supports their business interest and makes their family an economically viable unit. However, married brothers remain united so long business remains a joint venture. When it grows unwieldy, it gets bifurcated and consequently the family also separates. Generally there is a high degree of intra and inter familial co-operation in times of exigencies.

The Hindu Bannuwals have been traders and businessmen even prior to their migration. After their rehabilitation in Dehradun they continue to be the largest in business and trade. With their traditional acumen they could establish themselves gradually in business. They are now practically in every field right from vegetable venders to posh restaurant owners. There are among others cloth merchants, cycle and auto-parts dealers, transporters, pharmaceutical and electronic shop owners to name a few. In fact the bustling business complex at Premnagar is almost totally in the hands of these people who with their sheer hardwork, perseverance and endeavour could not only establish themselves in an area alien to them but have earned for themselves a special name as a major business community of the town.

The task of rehabilitation was not easy, as many had to face tremendous hardship with no financial support to reckon with. The government aid given to a few as compensation for the loss of property was too meager to be of any substantial help. To begin with, they picked up any odd job that came their way and lived in squalid congested camps which were allotted to the refugees. One of the informants narrated vividly about how he and his family members survived feeding on roasted Bengal grams for days together. He then started collecting fallen twigs and pieces of fuel wood from the jungle and sold it in the evening. He now proudly owns a popular tea stall. There is tremendous sense of the dignity of labour. Those who had flourishing business at Bannu had to do menial jobs for sheer sustenance. There were only few families who migrated to this place well in advance and with assistance from their wealthy relatives could start their business.

Though business continues to be their primary occupation but younger generation is aspiring for service in Government and private organisation and is also entering the white collared profession of law, medicine and engineering. However, for most cases it is difficult to just get out of the family business as there are pressures from within. Normally as soon as the son is able to do some accounting he is withdrawn from school and is persuaded to join the family enterprise. This leaves practically no time in the pursuit of higher learning. It is observed that women attain higher level of education that their menfolks for they continue to study upto graduate and post graduate level till they find a suitable match. It is seen that women, though are encouraged to seek jobs outside their home, do lend a helping hand in the manufacture of items of domestic use. Besides some do tailoring and knitting and contribute in small measures to the family budget. A few educated women are also in teaching professions.

There is a perceivable change in the attitude of the people towards women's education and the need for their emancipation. While the younger generation is more tolerant in their attitude and showing liberal trends towards allowing women more freedom, the older generation maintains that the true place for women is the home and that they should not be allowed to interfere in the men's domain.

As regards the religious beliefs, the Bannuwals show a fine blend of Sikh beliefs with Hindu religious practices. It is said that people of Bannu were greatly influenced by the teachings of the Sikh Gurus. Consequently Hindu and Sikh marriages take place. The Bannuwal household is a semblance of Hindu and Sikh faith. Within the same household some members follow Sikh faith while others follow the Hindu faith. After the partition and subsequently their repatriation to India, the people continue this tradition of mutual brotherhood and comradeship even till date. For instance the marriage ceremonies or life cycle rituals may be performed either in accordance with Hindu or Sikh religious rites. It is an accepted practice to dedicate usually the eldest child to the service of the Sikh Guru and accept the tenets of the Sikh faith.

Here it is pertinent to mention that in the wake of the terrorist violence of a particular community demanding a separate state there has been some erosion of faith between the members of the two communities. Some constraints are evident in their attitude towards each other. Marriages which were frequently solemnised between the members of the two groups are on the decline. Besides, people used to visit each others place of worship frequently but of late, this practice is also on the wane. At the same time it is heartening to note that people describe this as a passing phase.

On the political side, Bannuwals have formed their own association which undertakes welfare programmes for its people. For example, community halls are built and provided at a nominal fee to the members of the community to hold social ceremonies. Likewise utensils are also provided for such occasions. Financial and social assistance is also given to destitute women and poor widows. The association aims to enlarge its activities by opening free hospitals and medicine camps, generate employment opportunities for its unemployed youths, provide pension to old and needy people. However, all this required sufficient funds and resources which are obviously limited. At the time when this study was conducted an ambitious programme of publishing a directory of all the Bannuwal of Dehradun district was in the offing and when completed it will definitely prove to be of great worth in better organization and management of their society.

Bannuwals as a community are fully responsive to the changing needs of the time and have adapted themselves to the new modern styles of living. The older generation while accepting certain changes in their day to day living likes to dress up in their traditional *shalwar kameez* and *Pathan turban* which has become an insignia of the people of the Frontier. The younger generation, on the other hand, has moulded themselves to the modern western style of dressing.

While the community feeling is strong among the people of Bannu, they have always remained in cordial relationship with the local inhabitants. The dynamism of the people is worth recording for they have not only recovered from the trauma of partition but have been able to overcome successfully the most adverse phase of their history to cover a niche for themselves in an alien land. This perhaps is due only to their sheer grit, will power, remarkable ability of adjustment and adaptation to changing socio-political environment.

REFERENCE

Rose, H.A. (1919), *Glossary of the Tribes and Castes of the Punjab and North West Frontier Province,* Amar Prakashan Delhi, Vol. I and Vol. II. (Reprint).

INDEX

H

I

J

K

L

R

V

W

Y & Z